rock 'N' roll

rock
THE

rock 'N' roll
FAMOUS LYRICS

SCOTT BUCHANAN [EDITOR]

Harper Perennial

A Division of HarperCollinsPublishers

Rock 'n' Roll: The Famous Lyrics.

Copyright © 1994 by Scott Buchanan.

For information address:

HarperCollins Publishers, Inc.,

10 East 53rd Street, New York, New York 10022.

For

HarperCollins books may be purchased for educational, business, or sales promotional use. For information, please write to:

Special Markets Department, HarperCollins Publishers, Inc.,

10 East 53rd Street, New York, New York 10022.

First edition

Library of Congress Cataloging-in-Publication Data

Rock 'n' roll : the famous lyrics / by Scott Buchanan, editor. — 1st ed.

   p. cm.

  Includes indexes.

  ISBN 0-06-273235-8

  1. Rock music—Texts. I. Buchanan, Scott, 1954- . II. Title: Rock and roll.

ML54.6.R58 1994 [Case]

782.42166'0268—dc20   94-10112

                                         CIP

94 95 96 97 98 ◊/RED 10 9 8 7 6 5 4 3 2 1

He says,"Son can you play me a memory?
I'm not really sure how it goes
But it's sad and it's sweet and I knew it complete
When I wore a younger man's clothes."

PIANO MAN

BILLY JOEL

Mom,
   Dad, Steve, Patti, Victoria,
          and Jay

ontents

In a book like this one, there are a great many people who deserve recognition for their energies, opinions, and inspirations. In addition to my parents, Marilyn Buchanan and Bill Buchanan, my brother Steve, and my sister Patricia, I would like to thank the following associates and friends for their support: Lori Annaheim, Victoria McKernan, my agents Leigh Feldman and Liz Darhansoff, my editor Robert Wilson, Catherine Rafferty, Diane Zyats, Randi Martin,

Acknowledgments

Spencer Adams, Debby Johnston, Tony Schulte, Catherine Siewick, Oscar ``Smitty'' Herron, Chuck Bangert, Steve Chambers, Chris ``Cheebo'' Chevalier, Dan Connor, Michael Drapen, Doug Schleifer, Chris Walle, Kurt Roth, Ken Goldstein, Cathy Siciliano, Michael Oberman, and Jay Dallam.

> In addition to the wonderful songwriters included in this book, I am especially indebted to the wonderful people I have ``met'' in the music publishing industry for their generous cooperation and support. Without this support, this book truly would not have been possible. Much thanks to: Jack Rosner, Marsha Costa, Jeff Rosen, Jennifer Insogna, Barbara Carr, Ina Meibach, Cathy Gallagher, Scott Abrams, Anne Karle, Giny Bailey, Claudette Fergus, Becky Pommer-Jones, H. Patrick Meusel, Lisa Wills, Felicia Ronquillo, Doug Scott, Karen Adams, Gloria Boyce, Claire Johnston, Pamela Bendich, Diana Weller, Christine Rankin, Lester Boles, Helen Mallory, Dave Dillon, John Fishlock, Kelley Lynch, Elizabeth George, Robert Hunter, Annette Flowers, Mike Boila, John Courage, Wendy Welch, Ellen J. Burke, Alicia Winfield, Carole Broughton, Martin Cohen, Monte L. Morris, Robert Goodale, Len Freedman, James Calder, Joe Loomis, Don Warden, Michael Connelly, Kenny Young, Country Joe McDonald, Michael Goldsen, Robert Fitzpatrick, Felice Bryant, Lesslee Etzweiler, Stanley Mills, Keith Penney, Steven Weiss, C. Stamp, Tamaro Shad, Carol Carver, Brian Doyle, Marshal M. Gelfand, David Nelson, Nick Beu-Meir, John Massa, Eric Higginbottom, Randi V. Kantor, Garry Velletri, Sara Smith, B. Emerson, Deidre Baxter, Pegi Cecconi, Lirk Wentzell, Carla Goldby, Stuart Prager, and Michele Bourgerie.

> For their invaluable efforts and assistance in researching the owners of copyrights, I would like to thank Paul Casciani and the staff of BMI, as well as the staffs of ASCAP and PRS in London. This project may not have been possi-

9   ⟶ 10

ble without their generous help. I would also like to mention the BMI Foundation, Inc., and the wonderful work they do in support of young composers and creative programs for new music. I urge anyone interested in learning more about this group to contact The BMI Foundation, Inc., 320 West 57th Street, NY, NY 10019.

> For the ``flashbacks'' and other influential references, I would like to pay tribute to my reference books, including Joe Smith's *Off the Record*, Dick Jacobs's *Who Wrote That Song*, Art Spiegelman and Bob Schneider's *Whole Grains*, Dave Marsh's *The Heart of Rock and Soul*, all of the *Rolling Stone* encyclopedias, record guides, and interview books, John Hall's *The Sixties*, Norm Nite's *Rock On*, and Joel Whitburn's various *Billboard* books.

> I would also like to pay tribute to the greatest library in the world, the Library of Congress.

> And finally, I would like to thank Bill Fitzgerald, Kevin Murphy, Michael Oberman, and Helen Ashford for their assistance with the photographs.

A rock 'n' roll reference book? When I was growing up, I never thought rock 'n' roll would be around long enough to have a *history* book, much less a reference book. And if you had told me that there would be a Hall of Fame for rock stars or that rock songs would be piped into elevators and telephones, I would have asked for a hit of *your* pipe.

> Today, it is impossible to ignore the growing significance of rock 'n' roll music in mainstream American culture, and especially the continuing popularity of so-called ``classic rock.'' Just turn on your radio. Or open this book.

For almost four decades, rock and roll music has continued to influence the millions of people who have grown up listening to it. Popular rock lyrics have

Introduction

become the street poetry of our culture, part of the collective consciousness of the entire ``baby boomer'' generation.

> The goal of this book is to provide, for the first time ever, a comprehensive collection of the most famous and memorable rock 'n' roll quotes in a single easy-to-use reference, and to preserve this cultural record for posterity. It will not only celebrate and catalog much of the rock poetry of the period, but it will also give the reader a unique glimpse back to the attitudes, emotions, and images of their times.

> In this book you will discover and recall beautiful poetry, personal recollections, as well as an abundance of shared cultural memories. In addition to love and sex, issues and subjects contained in these pages include the Vietnam War, civil rights, assassinations, the environment, starvation, poverty, class wars, drugs, race, generational war, gender wars, homosexuality, cross-dressing, revolution, space exploration, anarchy, abortion, child abuse, gun control, the draft, hangovers, long hair, along with about a hundred entities that had never been heard of before or since.

> But is it fair to take the lyrics out of the song and document them in a way that was never intended? Because there is no way around it—rock lyrics were meant to be *heard* and not *seen*. To violate this truth by isolating one element of the whole work (print) without the rhythm and sound with which it was designed, leaves many of these lyrics awkward and vulnerable to simplistic criticism.

For what is fundamental to the magic of rock, if not its inaccessible nature? Mumbled words, secret messages, and electrical instrumentation were all important elements of the total rock language (as were cliches, repetition, and shouts).

> The people that declare some popular rock lyrics insignificant use the same kind of reasoning that people use when they complain that *Waiting for Godot* is "boring" theater and "nothing ever happens." They misunderstand the medium *and* the message. Like Beckett, rock lyricists instinctively recognize the strengths and weaknesses of language in their particular art form, and utilize this knowledge to express an *experience* that they intend. Language is often devalued and minimalized in an effort to expose its genuine limitations in modern life. That's not to say every lyric is a *Waiting for Godot* or even that every artist recognizes this effort, but the point is valid.

> It is certainly true that print can sometimes embarrass a lyric. But let it. This book is designed as a companion for participants in the rock 'n' roll experience, and not for critics of the art form.

> Anyway, rock 'n' roll has always meant more to its followers than the sum of its parts. It is a feeling, a notion, a view. This book, therefore, celebrates an important *part* of the rock legacy, and is dedicated to the faithful. Rock 'n' roll, like Christmas, exists on faith, tradition, and an imprecise memory. It's easy to see the sham and the commercialism, but impossible to ignore the profound feelings associated with its memory.

> Music, like dreams, mingles with your consciousness as well as your unconsciousness. It plays with your memory and stretches and reorganizes your thoughts and feelings in a most whimsical and personal way. It triggers memories and can anchor moments forever.

> So, if you've ever played *Wipeout* on a school desk or struggled to hit just the right note on an air guitar, step right in. These pages can be read—or sung—under a black light, a blue, rainy or marmalade sky, and most importantly, wherever you're alone with your thoughts. Laugh, smile, cry, frown, gag, and remember. And no apologies are necessary, when you read "Scuse me while I kiss the sky" and blurt out "Brehn de-denh, Denh dehn-dehn..."

To put it more bluntly, Yeah, Yeah, Yeah!

CRITERIA FOR SELECTION OF LYRICS

The selections for this edition cover the period from 1955–1984, and concentrate on the so-called "classic rock" songs (more or less). The next edition is planned to extend this coverage to 1994 and will include a lot more of the modern rock spinoffs as well as update the ongoing success of the artists in this book. I have tried to include what I feel most fans would expect to find here, at least in terms of representation.

➤ The goal of my selection process was not only to include the most popular and famous lyrics of rock 'n' roll, but also to try and represent most of the tastes of rock 'n' roll. While I'm sure the discerning fan will easily see which way my tastes lean, I have tried to include as many main entries (i.e., groups) as possible so that every rock fan would find something they are fond of here. And if you want to complain about the selections, send me better ones and I'll consider them in the next edition.

➤ The acquisition of permissions was perhaps the most frustrating part of the project. Although most of the publishers were extremely cooperative and understanding regarding my project, I never did find the publishers for some songs, and for others, the song publishers were unwilling to cooperate with the project. I apologize for these gaps, but am very proud for what *has* been achieved here. The glass is much more than half full and I have the songwriters and their publishers to thank (see Acknowledgments). Without their foresight and understanding of the special nature of this project, it surely would have been impossible to produce.

ORGANIZATION AND ARRANGEMENT

The arrangement of this book is designed to be simple and straightforward. Main entries are arranged alphabetically by Performer names. Under a Performer, entries are listed chronologically by year, then alphabetically by title within a year.

➤ Two indexes appear at the back of the book. All lyric entries can be accessed by the Song Title and Keyword Index; actual song titles are in italics. The Songwriter Index lists composers of the songs that appear in this book; arrangement is alphabetical by last name.

"Too Loud": That's what a Rhode Island school principal declared when these future hippies showed up for class in madras slacks. The boys were instructed to report to school the following day in more appropriate attire. Bell bottoms?

AP/WIDE WORLD PHOTOS

rock 'N' roll

AC/DC

Hey mama, look at me

I'm on my way to the Promised Land

I'm on the Highway to Hell

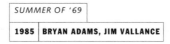

HIGHWAY TO HELL	
1979	ANGUS YOUNG, MALCOLM YOUNG, BON SCOTT

Bryan Adams

But when I look back now

The summer seemed to last forever…

Those were the best days of my life

SUMMER OF '69	
1985	BRYAN ADAMS, JIM VALLANCE

Aerosmith

Sing with me, sing for the years

Sing for the laughter'n sing for the tears

DREAM ON	
1973	STEVEN TYLER

Allman Brothers

Lord I was born a ramblin' man

Tryin' to make a living and doing the best I can

When it's time to leave I hope you'll understand

That I was born a ramblin' man

RAMBLIN' MAN	
1973	RICHARD BETTS

The Amboy Dukes

Come along if you care

Come along if you dare

Take a ride to the land inside of your mind

But please realize, you'll probably be surprised

For in the land unknown to man

Where fantasy is fact

So if you can, please understand

You might not come back

JOURNEY TO THE CENTER OF YOUR MIND	
1968	TED NUGENT, STEVE FARMER

America

Ain't the years gone by fast

I suppose you have missed them

Oh, I almost forgot to ask

Did you hear of my enlistment?

SANDMAN	
1971	DEWEY BUNNELL

The heat was hot and the ground was dry

But the air was full of sound

I've been through the desert on a horse with no name

It felt good to be out of the rain

A HORSE WITH NO NAME	
1972	DEWEY BUNNELL

But Oz never did give nothing to the Tin Man

That he didn't, didn't already have

And Cause never was a reason for the evening

Or the Tropic of Sir Galahad

TIN MAN	
1974	DEWEY BUNNELL

Well I tried to make it Sunday

But I got so damned depressed

That I set my sights on Monday

And I got myself undressed

SISTER GOLDEN HAIR	
1975	DEWEY BUNNELL

American Breed

Bend me, shape me, any way you want me

Long as you love me, it's alright

BEND ME, SHAPE ME	
1967	SCOTT ENGLISH, LAURENCE WEISS

The Angels

My boyfriend's back, he's gonna save my reputation

If I were you I'd take a permanent vacation

MY BOYFRIEND'S BACK	
1963	ROBERT FELDMAN, GERALD GOLDSTEIN

The Animals

There is a house in New Orleans

They call the Rising Sun

And it's been the ruin of many a poor boy

And God, I know, I'm one

HOUSE OF THE RISING SUN	
1964	TRADITIONAL, ALAN PRICE

Baby, do you understand me now

Sometimes I feel a little mad...

I'm just a soul whose intentions are good

Oh Lord, please don't let me be misunderstood

DON'T LET ME BE MISUNDERSTOOD	
1965	BENNIE BENJAMIN, SOL MARCUS, GLORIA CALDWELL

It's a hard world to get a break in

All the good things have been taken...

IT'S MY LIFE	
1965	ROGER ATKINS, CARL D'ERRICO

In this dirty old part of the city

Where the sun refused to shine

People tell me there ain't no use in tryin'

WE GOTTA GET OUT OF THIS PLACE	
1965	CYNTHIA WEILL, BARRY MANN

Strobe lights beam, creates dreams

Walls move, minds do too

On a warm San Franciscan night

SAN FRANCISCAN NIGHTS	
1967	ERIC BURDON, VICTOR BRIGGS, JOHNNY WEIDER, BARRY JENKINS, DANNY MCCULLOCH

you don't like what you're
you can always pick up
needle and move to
another groove. ● TIMOTHY LEARY

You wanna find the truth in life?

Don't pass music by

MONTEREY	
1968	ERIC BURDON, VICTOR BRIGGS, JOHNNY WEIDER, BARRY JENKINS, DANNY MCCULLOCH

Soon there'll be blood and many will die

Mothers and fathers back home they will cry...

Sky Pilot, How high can you fly?

SKY PILOT	
1968	ERIC BURDON, VICTOR BRIGGS, JOHNNY WEIDER, BARRY JENKINS, DANNY MCCULLOCH

Argent

And if they stare

Just let them burn their eyes on your movement...

Hold your head up, hold your head high

HOLD YOUR HEAD UP	
1972	ROD ARGENT, CHRIS WHITE

The Association

And when the masquerade is played and neighbor folks

Make jokes at who is most to blame today

ALONG COMES MARY	
1965	TANDYN ALMER

Who's tripping down the streets of the city...

Who's reaching out to capture a moment

Everyone knows it's Windy

WINDY	
1967	RUTHANN FRIEDMAN

Atlanta Rhythm Section

Imaginary lover, never disagree

Imaginary lover, you're mine anytime

IMAGINARY LOVER	
1978	BUDDY BUIE, ROBERT NIX, DEAN DAUGHERTY

Bad Company

It's why they call me Bad Company

And I can't deny

Bad Company, till the day I die

BAD COMPANY	
1974	PAUL RODGERS, SIMON KIRKE

Turn on your light

And stay with me a-while

And ease your worried mind

ROCK STEADY	
1974	**PAUL RODGERS**

Johnny was a schoolboy

When he heard his first Beatle song

"Love Me Do" I think it was and

From there it didn't take him long

Don't ya know that you are a

shooting star. Don't ya

know. Hey

Don't ya know that you

are a shooting star.

And all the world will love you

Just as long, as long as you are

SHOOTING STAR	
1974	**PAUL RODGERS**

Bachman-Turner Overdrive

You can see the morning but I can see the light

Try, try, try to let it ride...

LET IT RIDE	
1973	**RANDY BACHMAN, CHARLES TURNER**

So I took what I could get

And then she looked at me with those big brown eyes

And said, "You ain't seen nothing yet."

YOU AIN'T SEEN NOTHING YET	
1974	**RANDY BACHMAN**

21

⟶ 22

The Band

I pulled into Nazareth, was feelin' 'bout half past dead

I just need some place where I can lay my head

"Hey mister can you tell me where a man might find a bed?"

He just grinned and shook my hand, and "No" was all he said

Take a load off Fanny

Take a load for free…

And you put the load right on me

THE WEIGHT	
1968, 1970	J. ROBBIE ROBERTSON

I swear by the mud below my feet

You can't raise a Caine back up

When he's in defeat

THE NIGHT THEY DROVE OLD DIXIE DOWN	
1969	J. ROBBIE ROBERTSON

Up on Cripple Creek she sends me…

I don't have to speak she defends me

A drunkard's dream if I ever did see one

UP ON CRIPPLE CREEK	
1969	J. ROBBIE ROBERTSON

Save your neck or save your brother

Looks like it's one or the other

Oh you don't know the shape I'm in

THE SHAPE I'M IN	
1970	J. ROBBIE ROBERTSON

Your brow is sweatin' and your mouth is dry

Fancy people go drifting by

STAGE FRIGHT	
1970	J. ROBBIE ROBERTSON

Beach Boys

Little surfer, little one

Make my heart come all undone

Catch a wave and you're sittin' on top of the world

Well I'm not braggin', babe, so don't put me down

But I've got the fastest set of wheels in town

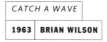

If everybody had an ocean

Across the U.S.A.

Then ev'rybody'd be surfin'

Like Cal-i-for-ni-a

Well, it's been building up inside of me for

Oh, I don't know how long

And she'll have fun, fun, fun

Till her daddy takes the T-Bird away

Round, round get around, I get around

I GET AROUND	
1964	**BRIAN WILSON**

There's a world where I can go

And tell my secrets to

In my room

IN MY ROOM	
1964	**BRIAN WILSON AND GARY USHER**

Will I look for the same things in a woman

That I did in a girl?

WHEN I GROW UP (TO BE A MAN)	
1964	**BRIAN WILSON**

Well East coast girls are hip

I really dig those styles they wear...

I wish they all could be California girls

CALIFORNIA GIRLS	
1965	**BRIAN WILSON**

If you should ever leave me

Life would still go on, believe me

GOD ONLY KNOWS	
1966	**TONY ASHER, BRIAN WILSON**

I love the colorful clothes she wears

And the way the sunlight plays upon her hair...

I'm picking up good vibrations

GOOD VIBRATIONS	
1966	**BRIAN WILSON AND MIKE LOVE**

Those

Wouldn't it be nice if we were older

Then we wouldn't have to wait so long

WOULDN'T IT BE NICE	
1966	BRIAN WILSON AND TONY ASHER

Beatles

Well shake it up baby

Twist and shout

TWIST AND SHOUT	
1962	BERT RUSSELL, PHIL MEDLEY

The decision was to let me be strong, or to bring him in and make the group stronger. I decided to make the group stronger.

JOHN LENNON ON BRINGING PAUL MCCARTNEY INTO THE PRE-BEATLES QUARRY MEN.

in the cheaper seats clap. The rest of you rattle your jewelry

JOHN LENNON, IN A BEATLES' PERFORMANCE AT THE ROYAL VARIETY PERFORMANCE, 11/15/63

I'll tell you something

I think you'll understand

I WANT TO HOLD YOUR HAND	
1963	JOHN LENNON, PAUL MCCARTNEY

It's been a hard day's night

And I've been working like a dog

HARD DAY'S NIGHT	
1964	JOHN LENNON, PAUL MCCARTNEY

I'm a loser

and I'm not what I appear to be

I'M A LOSER	
1964	JOHN LENNON, PAUL MCCARTNEY

25

⟶ 26

Visually they are a nightmare:
Beatnik suits and great pudding
they are a near disaster: gui
a merciless beat that does away
mony and melody. Their ly-
shouts of yeah, yeah, yeah,
preposterous farrago of

The Fab Four meet the press at the Waldorf-
Astoria in New York. AP/WIDE WORLD PHOTOS

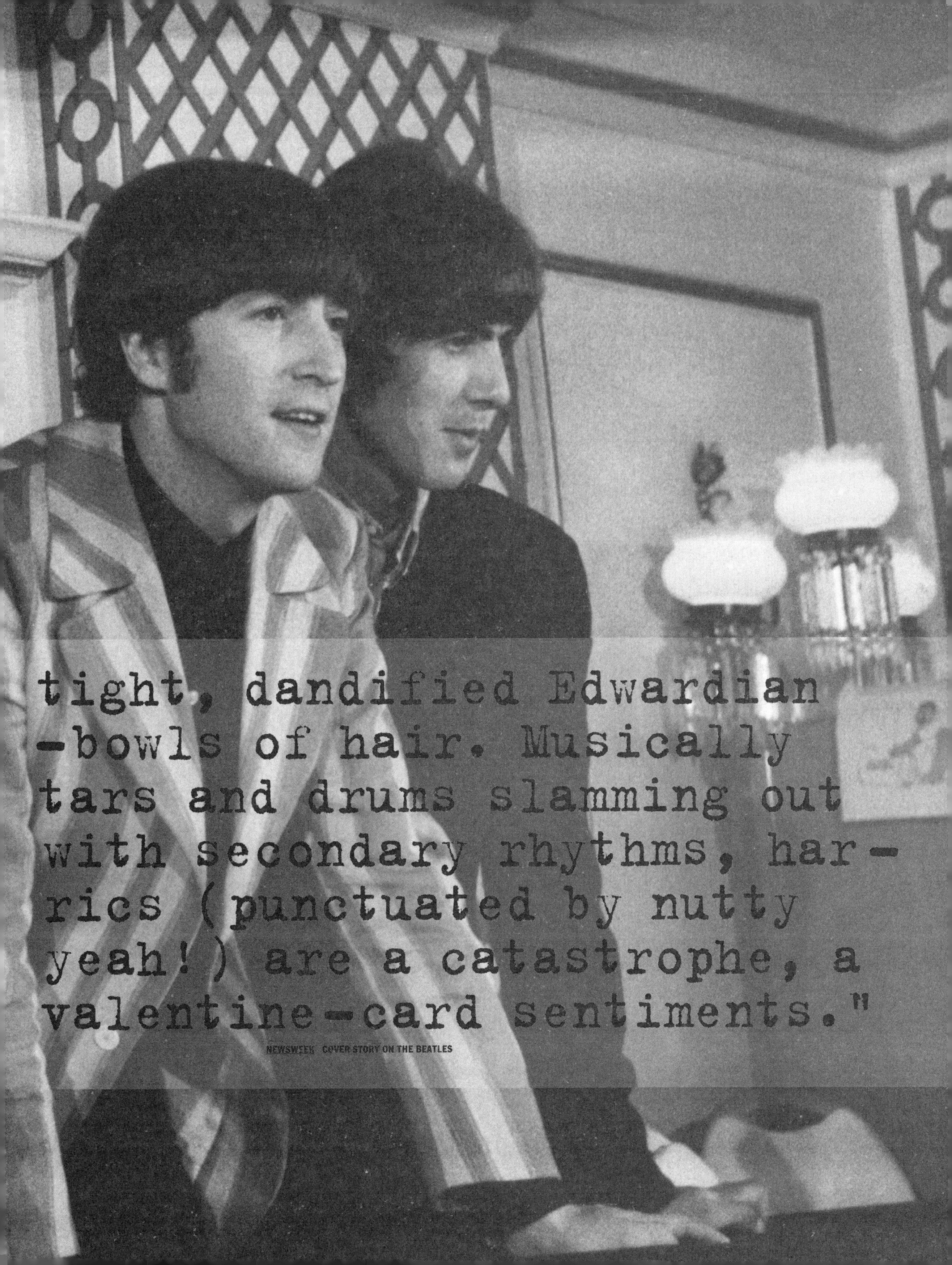

tight, dandified Edwardian
-bowls of hair. Musically
tars and drums slamming out
with secondary rhythms, har-
rics (punctuated by nutty
yeah!) are a catastrophe, a
valentine-card sentiments."

NEWSWEEK COVER STORY ON THE BEATLES

Well she was just seventeen

And you know what I mean

I SAW HER STANDING THERE	
1964	JOHN LENNON, PAUL MCCARTNEY

She loves you (yeah, yeah, yeah)

SHE LOVES YOU	
1964	JOHN LENNON, PAUL MCCARTNEY

I don't care too much for money

Money can't buy me love

CAN'T BUY ME LOVE	
1965	JOHN LENNON, PAUL MCCARTNEY

She's a big teaser

She took me half the way there...

She was a day tripper

DAY TRIPPER	
1965	JOHN LENNON, PAUL MCCARTNEY

The Beatles,
their own
ments—counter

She's the kind of girl you want so much

It makes you sorry

Still you don't regret a single day

GIRL	
1965	JOHN LENNON, PAUL MCCARTNEY

Help! I need somebody

Help! Not just any body

Help! You know I need someone

HELP!	
1965	JOHN LENNON, PAUL MCCARTNEY

We're all alone and there's nobody else

You still moan "Keep your hands to yourself"

I'm down

I'M DOWN	
1965	**JOHN LENNON, PAUL MCCARTNEY**

Love has a nasty habit of disappearing overnight...

Your voice is soothing, but the words aren't clear

I'M LOOKING THROUGH YOU	
1965	**JOHN LENNON, PAUL MCCARTNEY**

Though I know I'll never lose affection

For people and things that went before

I know I'll often stop and think about them

IN MY LIFE	
1965	**JOHN LENNON, PAUL MCCARTNEY**

who like many of the new groups write
music, have added interesting embellish-
point, madrigal effects, tonal progres-
sions, which are so adroitly done
that musicologists openly wonder if
the British lads know what on earth
they are doing.

LIFE MAGAZINE, 1965

I once had a girl

Or should I say she once had me

NORWEGIAN WOOD (THIS BIRD HAS FLOWN)	
1965	**JOHN LENNON, PAUL MCCARTNEY**

We're more popular than, which will go first—rock n

JOHN LENNON, IN AN INTERVIEW PUBLISHED IN THE LONDON EVENING STANDARD, MARCH 4, 1966

Most of the ballady stuff
own...although I did bring
John for help with the
could always spot a bum

Doesn't have a point of view

Knows not where he's going to

Isn't he a bit like you and me?

NOWHERE MAN	
1965	JOHN LENNON, PAUL MCCARTNEY

She's got a ticket to ride

But she don't care

TICKET TO RIDE	
1965	JOHN LENNON, PAUL MCCARTNEY

You're telling all those lies

About the good things we can have

If we close our eyes

THINK FOR YOURSELF	
1965	GEORGE HARRISON

Life is very short, and there's no time

for fussing and fighting, my friend

WE CAN WORK IT OUT	
1965	JOHN LENNON, PAUL MCCARTNEY

Yesterday, all my troubles seemed so far away

Now it looks as though they're here to stay

Oh I believe in yesterday

YESTERDAY	
1965	JOHN LENNON, PAUL MCCARTNEY

There's nothing you can make that can't be made

No one you can save that can't be saved

ALL YOU NEED IS LOVE	
1966	JOHN LENNON, PAUL MCCARTNEY

Jesus now. I don't know roll or Christianity.

I wrote on my "Eleanor Rigby" to third verse. John line. **PAUL McCARTNEY**

Ultimately, the Beatles are second to none in all departments. I don't think there has ever been a better song written than "Eleanor Rigby."

JERRY LEIBER ON SONGWRITING

All the lonely people

Where do they all come from?...

Where do they all belong?

ELEANOR RIGBY	
1966	**JOHN LENNON, PAUL McCARTNEY**

Your day breaks...

You find that all her words of kindness

Linger on when she no longer needs you

FOR NO ONE	
1966	**JOHN LENNON, PAUL McCARTNEY**

When I'm in the middle of a dream...

Please don't wake me no, don't shake me

I'M ONLY SLEEPING	
1966	**JOHN LENNON, PAUL McCARTNEY**

Dear Sir or Madam will you read my book

It took me years to write will you take a look

PAPERBACK WRITER	
1966	**JOHN LENNON, PAUL McCARTNEY**

Can you hear me that when it rains and shines

It's just a state of mind

RAIN	
1966	**JOHN LENNON, PAUL McCARTNEY**

She said I know what it's like to be dead...

And she's making me feel

Like I've never been born

SHE SAID SHE SAID	
1966	**JOHN LENNON, PAUL McCARTNEY**

Now my advice for those who die

Declare the pennies on your eye!

Cause I'm the taxman

TAXMAN	
1966	GEORGE HARRISON

Groups with guitars are on

Turn off your mind, relax, and float downstream

It is not dying

TOMORROW NEVER KNOWS	
1966	GEORGE HARRISON

Found my way upstairs and had a smoke

Somebody spoke and I went into a dream

I'd love to turn you on

A DAY IN THE LIFE	
1967	JOHN LENNON, PAUL MCCARTNEY

How does it feel to be one of the beautiful people?

Now that you know who you are

What do you want to be?...

What did you see when you were there?

Nothing that doesn't show

BABY YOU'RE A RICH MAN	
1967	JOHN LENNON, PAUL MCCARTNEY

There's a fog upon L.A.

And my friends have lost their way

BLUE JAY WAY	
1967	GEORGE HARRISON

the way out.

DECCA (LTD.) RECORDS EXECUTIVE AFTER CANCELLATION OF A BEATLES AUDITION IN 1961.

The Beatles live at Shea Stadium, 1966.

UPI/BETTMANN NEWSPHOTOS

I'm fixing a hole where the rain gets in

And stops my mind from wandering

Where it will go

FIXING A HOLE	
1967	**JOHN LENNON, PAUL MCCARTNEY**

Day after day, alone on a hill

The man with the foolish grin

Is keeping perfectly still

THE FOOL ON THE HILL	
1967	**JOHN LENNON, PAUL MCCARTNEY**

I am the walrus, goo goo goojoob

I AM THE WALRUS	
1967	**JOHN LENNON, PAUL MCCARTNEY**

Picture yourself in a boat on a river

With tangerine trees and marmalade

Skies

LUCY IN THE SKY WITH DIAMONDS	
1967	JOHN LENNON, PAUL MCCARTNEY

A pretty nurse is selling poppies from a tray

And tho she feels as if she's in a play

She is anyway

PENNY LANE	
1967	JOHN LENNON, PAUL MCCARTNEY

They've been going in and out of style

But they're guaranteed to raise a smile...

SERGEANT PEPPER'S LONELY HEARTS CLUB BAND	
1967	JOHN LENNON, PAUL MCCARTNEY

Living is easy with eyes closed

Misunderstanding all you see

It's getting hard to be someone

STRAWBERRY FIELDS FOREVER	
1967	JOHN LENNON, PAUL MCCARTNEY

(What do you see when you turn out the light?)

I can't tell you but I know it's mine

WITH A LITTLE HELP FROM MY FRIENDS	
1967	JOHN LENNON, PAUL MCCARTNEY

Words are flying out like endless rain into a paper cup

ACROSS THE UNIVERSE	
1968	JOHN LENNON, PAUL MCCARTNEY

The
ration
that brought
a sort

Ev'rybody's got something to hide

Except for me and my monkey

EVERYBODY'S GOT SOMETHING TO HIDE EXCEPT FOR ME AND MY MONKEY	
1968	**JOHN LENNON, PAUL McCARTNEY**

Looking through the bent backed tulips

To see how the other half live

Looking through a glass onion...

GLASS ONION	
1968	**JOHN LENNON, PAUL McCARTNEY**

She's not a girl who misses much...

I need a fix 'cause I'm going down

HAPPINESS IS A WARM GUN	
1968	**JOHN LENNON, PAUL McCARTNEY**

Do you, don't you want me to love you?

I'm coming down fast, but I'm miles above you

HELTER SKELTER	
1968	**JOHN LENNON, PAUL McCARTNEY**

Hey Jude, don't let me down

You have found her, now go and get her

HEY JUDE	
1968	**JOHN LENNON, PAUL McCARTNEY**

**Everywhere we looked was change.
Beatles brought a new music to a gene-
hungry for it...and the television
it into the living room evolved into
of national nervous system.**

TOM WICKER IN THE SIXTIES

I'd give you every thing I've got

For a little peace of mind

I'M SO TIRED

1968 | JOHN LENNON, PAUL MCCARTNEY

Sexy Sadie what have you done

You made a fool of everyone

SEXY SADIE

1968 | JOHN LENNON, PAUL MCCARTNEY

You know how hard it can be

The way things are going

They're going to crucify me

THE BALLAD OF JOHN AND YOKO

1969 | JOHN LENNON, PAUL MCCARTNEY

Temperature's rising, fever is high

Can't see no future, can't see no sky...

COLD TURKEY

1969 | JOHN LENNON, PAUL MCCARTNEY

One thing I can tell you is you got to be free

Come together, right now, over me

COME TOGETHER

1969 | JOHN LENNON, PAUL MCCARTNEY

Sweet Loretta Modern thought she was a woman

But she was another man...

Get back to where you once belonged

GET BACK

1969 | JOHN LENNON, PAUL MCCARTNEY

Ev'rybody's talking about:

Bagism, Shagism, Dragism, Madism, Ragism, Tagism

All we are saying is give peace a chance

GIVE PEACE A CHANCE	
1969	JOHN LENNON, PAUL MCCARTNEY

Mean Mister Mustard sleeps in the park

Shaves in the dark trying to save paper

MEAN MR. MUSTARD	
1969	JOHN LENNON, PAUL MCCARTNEY

You say you want a revolution...

But when you talk about destruction

Don't you know that you can count me out

REVOLUTION	
1969	JOHN LENNON, PAUL MCCARTNEY

She came in through the bathroom window,

Protected by a silver spoon

SHE CAME IN THROUGH THE BATHROOM WINDOW	
1969	JOHN LENNON, PAUL MCCARTNEY

Somewhere in her smile she knows

That I don't need no other lover

SOMETHING	
1969	GEORGE HARRISON

And when the broken-hearted people

Living in the world agree

There will be an answer

LET IT BE	
1970	JOHN LENNON, PAUL MCCARTNEY

I'd like to say thank you on behalf of the group and our- selves, and I hope we passed the audition.

JOHN LENNON, AT THE CONCLUSION OF THE BEATLES' LAST "LIVE" PERFORMANCE ON THE ROOFTOP OF THE ABBEY ROAD STUDIO IN LONDON IN 1969,
AS CAPTURED ON THE ALBUM, "LET IT BE"

The bigger we got, the more unreality we had to face... It happened bit by bit, gradually, until this com- plete craziness is surrounding you, and you re doing exactly what you don t want to do with people you can t stand—the people you hated when you were ten. JOHN LENNON

The Bee Gees

Do you know what it's like on the outside?

Don't go talking too loud

You'll cause a landslide Mister Jones

NEW YORK MINING DISASTER—1941	
1967	**BARRY GIBB, ROBIN GIBB**

There you go with your fancy lies...

With all your jive talkin, you're tellin' me lies

JIVE TALKIN'	
1975	**BARRY GIBB, ROBIN GIBB, MAURICE GIBB**

Archie Bell and the Drells

Hi, everybody. I'm Archie Bell of the Drells, of Houston, Texas.

We don't only sing, we dance just as good as we want.

TIGHTEN UP	
1968	**ARCHIE BELL, BILLY BUTLER**

It's undoubtedly the only record ever to hit Number One while its lead vocalist was recovering from a wound received in Vietnam.

DAVE MARSH, IN A DISCUSSION ABOUT "TIGHTEN UP" IN HIS BOOK <u>THE HEART OF ROCK AND SOUL</u>

Pat Benatar

Your love has set my soul on fire

But it's out of control

HEARTBREAKER	
1979	**GEOFF GILL, CLIFF WADE**

Be a good little boy and you get a new toy

Tell grandma you fell off the swing...

HELL IS FOR CHILDREN	
1980	**N. GERALDO, PAT BENATAR, R. CAPPS**

The critical
point in lis-
tening comes
when a girl
becomes old
enough to feel
serious inter-
est in a boy.
When she is
pinned, when
her big inter-
est goes from
the group to
just one boy,
then she starts
losing interest
in rock 'n'
roll. She wants
to stop dancing
by herself, and
start dancing
with this one
boy—in his
arms—and to
regular dance
music. By the
time most kids
are high school
seniors their
interest in
rock 'n' roll is
either gone or
usually on the
wane. • CLYDE WALLACH, LOS
ANGELES RECORD STORE OWNER, 1965

You're a real tough cookie with a long history

Of breaking little hearts like the one in me

HIT ME WITH YOUR BEST SHOT	
1980	E. SCHWARTZ

George Benson

Are we really happy with this lonely game we play

Looking for words to say?...

We're lost in this masquerade

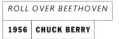

MASQUERADE	
1972	LEON RUSSELL

Chuck Berry

Oh Mabellene why can't you be true

You've started back doin' the things you used to do

MABELLENE	
1955	CHUCK BERRY, RUSS FRATTO

Roll over Beethoven and tell Tchaikovsky the news

ROLL OVER BEETHOVEN	
1956	CHUCK BERRY

It's gotta be Rock and Roll Music

If you wanna dance with me

ROCK AND ROLL MUSIC	
1957	CHUCK BERRY

Who'd never ever learned to read or write so well

But he could play a guitar just like a-ringin' a bell

JOHNNY B. GOODE	
1958	CHUCK BERRY

Don't bother me, leave me alone

Anyway, I'm almost grown

ALMOST GROWN	
1959	**CHUCK BERRY**

Yes, I'm so glad I'm livin' in the U.S.A.

Anything you got, we got it right here in the U.S.A.

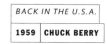

BACK IN THE U.S.A.	
1959	**CHUCK BERRY**

And I woke up high over Albuquerque

On a jet to the Promised Land...

Tell the folks back home this is the Promised Land

Callin' and the poor boy's on the line

THE PROMISED LAND	
1964	**CHUCK BERRY**

Tell Tchaikovsky the news:

Chuck Berry in concert.

AP/WIDE WORLD PHOTOS

⟶ 42

As I got on a city bus and found a vacant seat

I thought I saw my future bride walkin' up the street...

Nadine, Honey is that you

Oh Nadine, Honey, is that you?

Seems like ev'ry time I see you darlin'

You got somethin' else to do

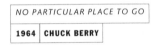

NADINE (IS IT YOU?)

1964 | CHUCK BERRY

Riding along in my automobile

My baby beside me at the wheel

I stole a kiss at the turn of a mile

My curiosity running wild

Cruising and playing the radio

With No Particular Place to Go

NO PARTICULAR PLACE TO GO

1964 | CHUCK BERRY

Sometimes I will, then again, I think I won't...

We were reelin' and a rockin' and rollin'

Till the break of dawn

REELIN' AND ROCKIN'

1965 | CHUCK BERRY

Those of you who will not sing

You must be playin' with your own Ding-A-Ling

MY DING-A-LING

1972 | CHUCK BERRY

What fun those darn drugs were. Marvelous
wobble in the middle of a civilization

The Big Bopper

Ain't-a nothin' in the world like a big-eyed girl

Make me act so funny, make me spend my money

Make me feel real loose like a long-neck goose

Oh baby, that's what I like

CHANTILLY LACE	
1958	**J. P. RICHARDSON**

Big Brother and the Holding Company

Take it

Take another little piece of my heart now baby...

You know you got it if it makes you feel good

PIECE OF MY HEART	
1967	**BERT BERNS, JERRY RAGAVOY**

Black Sabbath

Nobody wants him, they just turn their heads...

Nobody helps him, now he has his revenge

IRON MAN	
1970	**ANTHONY LOMMI, JOHN OSBORNE, WILLIAM WARD, TERENCE BUTLER**

Happiness I cannot feel

So love to me is so unreal

PARANOID	
1970	**ANTHONY LOMMI, JOHN OSBORNE, WILLIAM WARD, TERENCE BUTLER**

Blind Faith

I'm wasted and I can't find my way home

CAN'T FIND MY WAY HOME	
1969	**STEVE WINWOOD**

worlds aslant, a personal speed
equally out of control.

THOMAS MCGUANE, IN HIS BOOK "NOTHING BUT BLUE SKIES"

I have finally found a place to live

In the presence of the Lord

PRESENCE OF THE LORD

| 1969 | **ERIC CLAPTON** |

Blondie

We knew each other well

Although we never met

Messages passed to tell, equal respect

ENGLISH BOYS

| 1982 | **DEBORAH HARRY, CHRIS STEIN** |

Blood, Sweat, and Tears

I can swear there ain't no heaven

And I pray there ain't no hell

AND WHEN I DIE

| 1966 | **LAURA NYRO** |

Talkin' 'bout your troubles, it's a cryin' sin

Ride a painted pony, let the spinning wheel spin

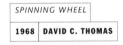

SPINNING WHEEL

| 1968 | **DAVID C. THOMAS** |

Blue Cheer

Well I called my congressman, he said quote

"I'd like to help you son, but you're too young to vote"

SUMMERTIME BLUES

| 1958 | **EDDIE COCHRAN, JERRY CAPEHART** |

Blue Oyster Cult

Forty thousand men and women every day

We can be like they are

Come on baby, don't fear the reaper

(DON'T FEAR) THE REAPER

| 1976 | **DONALD ROESER** |

Blues Image

Ride captain ride upon your mystery ship

Be amazed at the friends you're having on your trip

RIDE CAPTAIN RIDE	
1970	FRANK KONTE

Boston

So many people have come and gone

Their faces fade as the years go by

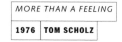

MORE THAN A FEELING	
1976	TOM SCHOLZ

I'm sure a psychologist would have an answer right away, but it doesn't matter what it is or how little a project it is. If it's just writing a short letter to some one, I always end up tearing it up, doing it again and not liking it—spending hours at something that should take 20 minutes. TOM SCHOLZ, ON WHY HE TAKES SO LONG TO FINISH ALBUMS

I understand about indecision

I don't care about getting behind...

All I want is to have my peace of mind

PEACE OF MIND	
1976	TOM SCHOLZ

Well I'm taking my time, I'm just movin' along

You'll forget about me after I've been gone

LONG TIME	
1976	TOM SCHOLZ

David Bowie

This is Major Tom to ground control

I'm stepping thro' the door

And I'm floating in a most peculiar way

And the stars look very different today

For here am I floating in a tin can

Far above the world

Planet Earth is blue

And there's nothing I can do

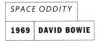

SPACE ODDITY

1969 | **DAVID BOWIE**

'Cause I'd rather stay here

With all the madmen

Than perish with the sadmen running free

And I'd rather play here with all the madmen

For I'm quite content, they're all as sane as me

ALL THE MADMEN

1971 | **DAVID BOWIE**

So I turned myself to face me

But I've never caught a glimpse

Of how the others must see the faker

I'm much too fast to take that test

Ch-ch-ch-ch-changes, turn and face the strange

Don't wanna be a richer man

It's gonna have to be a diff'rent man

Time may change me, but I can't trace time...

Oh look out you rockin' rollers

Pretty soon now you're gonna get older...

I watch the ripples change their size

But never leave the stream of warm impermanence

And so the days flow thru my eyes

But still the days seem the same

CHANGES

1971, 1973 | **DAVID BOWIE**

David Bowie performing at
Radio City Music Hall, 1974.

Rebel, rebel, you've torn your dress

Rebel, rebel your face is a mess

Rebel, rebel, how could they know

Hot tramp, I love you so

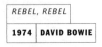

REBEL, REBEL	
1974	DAVID BOWIE

It wasn't just peer pressure. To get access to youth culture you had to get high. Without grass, you were an outsider looking in.

Fame—What's your name?

FAME	
1975	DAVID BOWIE, JOHN LENNON, CARLOS ALOMAR

Do you remember, President Nixon?

Do you remember the bills you have to pay

For even yesterday?

YOUNG AMERICAN	
1975	DAVID BOWIE

The Box Tops

Give me a ticket for an airplane

Ain't got time to take a fast train...

My baby just wrote me a letter

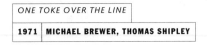

THE LETTER	
1967	WAYNE CARSON THOMPSON

Brewer and Shipley

Like everything else I've been through

It opened up my eyes

And now I'm one toke over the line, sweet Jesus

ONE TOKE OVER THE LINE	
1971	MICHAEL BREWER, THOMAS SHIPLEY

Arthur Brown

I am the God of Hellfire—and I bring you—Fire!!

	FIRE
1968	ARTHUR BROWN

Jackson Browne

Doctor, my eyes, tell me what is wrong

Was I unwise to leave them open for so long?

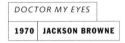

	DOCTOR MY EYES
1970	JACKSON BROWNE

When you see through love's illusions

There lies the danger

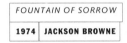

	FOUNTAIN OF SORROW
1974	JACKSON BROWNE

Though the years give way to uncertainty

And the fear of living for nothing strangles the will

	THE FUSE
1976	JACKSON BROWNE

Say a prayer for the pretender

Who started out so young and strong

Only to surrender

	THE PRETENDER
1976	JACKSON BROWNE

I look around for the friends I used to turn to...

Lookin' into their eyes I see them runnin' too

	RUNNING ON EMPTY
1978	JACKSON BROWNE

Go to class stoned. Shop for food stoned. Go to the movies stoned. See, all is transformed. The world just started again! And sex was ethereal. Did anybody ever do this before?

JOHN HALL IN "THE SIXTIES"

Under the neon light

Sellin' day for night

It's alright

DOWN ON THE BOULEVARD	
1980	JACKSON BROWNE

James Brown

Come here mama, and dig this crazy scene

Not too bad dad, but his line is pretty clean

I ain't no drag, Papa's Got a Brand New Bag

PAPA'S GOT A BRAND NEW BAG (PART 1)	
1965	JAMES BROWN

I don't care about your past

I just want our love to last

I don't care about your faults

I just want to satisfy your thoughts

When you kiss me, when you miss me...

I wake up in a cold sweat

COLD SWEAT	
1967	JAMES BROWN, ALFRED ELLIS

They call me the Godfather of soul.
business that nobody can fill my

You don't love nobody else. Get back

I can't stand myself, I can't stand my love

Good God

I CAN'T STAND MYSELF (WHEN YOU TOUCH ME)	
1967	JAMES BROWN

Sometimes I feel so nice (Good Lord)

I jump back, I want-a kiss myself

I got soul, and I'm superbad...

Right on, people, let it all hang out

It's God's
shoes. **JAMES BROWN**

> *CALL ME SUPERBAD*
>
> **1970 | JAMES BROWN**

Say it loud: "I'm Black and I'm Proud"

Some people say we got a lot of malice

Some say it's alot of nerve

But I say we won't stop movin'

Till we get what we deserve...

We're people, we're like the birds and the bees

But we'd rather die on our feet than keep living on our knees

Stay on the scene, get on up, like a sex machine...

The way I like it is the way it is

I got mine and I don't worry 'bout his

Get on up and shake your money maker

GET UP (I FEEL LIKE BEING A SEX MACHINE)	
1970	JAMES BROWN, BOBBY BYRD, RONALD LENHOFF

Thinkin' of losing that funky feeling, don't!

Cause you got to use what you got to get what you want!

Hot Pants! Smokin'!...

You walk just like you got The only lovin' left...

Bring it on one more, hit me

HOT PANTS	
1971	JAMES BROWN

Able to stop a riot
with a single

I'm a greedy man, I'm a greedy man

My name ain't Jody, but my name is Brown

I like to love, to get down, down, down

LINER NOTE ON A JAMES BROWN ALBUM

I'M A GREEDY MAN (PART 1)	
1971	JAMES BROWN, CHARLES BOBBITT

Tho we need it (Soul Power)

We got to have it (Soul Power)

Tho we want it (Soul Power)

Got to have it...

If I want to get under your skin

If I get there I have to win

If you need some soul

Come on and get some

And then you'll know where I'm coming from

Vio

SOUL POWER	
1971	JAMES BROWN

Like a dull knife, you just ain't cuttin'

You're just talkin' alot, just sayin' nothin'...

Don't tell me how to do my thing

When you can't do your own

TALKIN' LOUD AND SAYIN NOTHIN'	
1971	**JAMES BROWN, BOBBY BYRD**

I say the long haired hippies and the Afro basket

All together when the clock strikes

And they party on the good foot

You know they dancin' on the good foot...

A whole lotta bills and m'money spent

And that's on m' bad foot

GET ON THE GOOD FOOT (PART 1)	
1972	**JAMES BROWN, FRED WESLEY, JOE MIMS**

"Uhnh".

Yeah, yeah, yeah

Yeah, yeah, yeah

Popcorn

Some like 'em fat, some like 'em tall

Some like 'em short, skinny legs and all

MOTHER POPCORN (YOU GOT TO HAVE A MOTHER FOR ME—PART 1)	
1973	**JAMES BROWN, ALFRED ELLIS**

lence is as American as cherry pie.

H. RAP BROWN

Brownsville Station

Checkin' out the halls makin' sure the coast is clear

Lookin' in the stalls, no, there ain't nobody here...

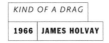

SMOKIN' IN THE BOYS ROOM	
1973	MICHAEL RODA, MICHAEL LUTZ

Buckinghams

Kind of a drag, when you're baby don't love you

Kind of a drag, when you know she's been untrue

KIND OF A DRAG	
1966	JAMES HOLVAY

Hey baby they're playing our song

The one we used to play when we used to get along

HEY BABY (THEY'RE PLAYIN' OUR SONG)	
1967	JIM HOLVAY, GARY BEISBER

My baby, she's made out of love

Like one of those bunnies at the Playboy Club

MERCY, MERCY, MERCY	
1967	GAIL LEVY, VINCENT LEVY

Buffalo Springfield

There's something happening here

What it is ain't exactly clear

FOR WHAT IT'S WORTH	
1966, 1967	STEPHEN STILLS

Oh hello, Mister Soul,

I dropped by to pick up a reason

MR. SOUL	
1967	NEIL YOUNG

Buffalo Springfield performing on television.

L\R: Dewey Martin, Richie Furay, Stephen

Stills, Jim Fielder, Neil Young.

Roger McGuinn and David Crosby of the Byrds.

Jimmy Buffett

Heading out to San Francisco...

I got my hush puppies on

I guess I never was meant for glitter rock and roll

COME MONDAY	
1974	**JIMMY BUFFETT**

All of the faces and all of the places

Wondering where they'd all disappeared

CHANGES IN LATITUDES, CHANGES IN ATTITUDES	
1976	**JIMMY BUFFETT**

Wasting away in Margaritaville

Searching for my lost shaker of salt

MARGARITAVILLE	
1976	**JIMMY BUFFETT**

The Buoys

Hungry as hell no food to eat...

Timothy, Timothy, where on earth did you go?

Timothy, Timothy, God why don't I know?

TIMOTHY	
1970	**RUPERT HOLMES**

The Byrds

I'll probably feel a whole lot better

When you're gone

I'LL FEEL A WHOLE LOT BETTER	
1965	**GENE CLARK**

There is a season, turn, turn, turn

And a time to every purpose under heaven

A time to gain, a time to lose

A time to rend, a time to sew

A time for love, a time for hate

A time for peace, I swear it's not too late.

TURN, TURN, TURN	
1965	PETE SEEGER, ADAPTED FROM THE BOOK OF ECCLESIASTES

Eight miles high, and when you touch down

You'll find that it's stranger than known

Signs in the street that say where you're going

Are somewhere just being their own

EIGHT MILES HIGH	
1966	GENE CLARK, DAVID CROSBY, JIM MCGUINN

Sacred cows make the tast hamburger.
A REMARK ATTRIBUTED TO ABBIE HOFFMAN, RECALLED AT HIS DEATH

A little bit of courage is all we lack...

I can recall a time when I wasn't ashamed

To reach out to a friend

GOIN' BACK	
1967	GERRY GOFFIN AND CAROLE KING

Then it's time to go downtown

Where the agent man won't let you down

Sell your soul to the company

Who are waiting there to sell plastic ware

And in a week or two

If you make the charts

The girls will tear you apart

SO YOU WANT TO BE ROCK 'N' ROLL STAR	
1967	JIM MCGUINN AND CHRIS HILLMAN

And if you think I'm ready

You may lead me to the chasm

Where the rivers of our vision flow into one another

WASN'T BORN TO FOLLOW	
1968	GERRY GOFFIN, CAROLE KING

The river flows, it flows to the sea

Wherever that river flows

That's where I want to be

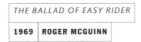

THE BALLAD OF EASY RIDER	
1969	ROGER MCGUINN

The Carpenters

What I've got they used to call the blues

Nothin' is really wrong

Feelin' like I don't belong

iest

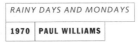

RAINY DAYS AND MONDAYS	
1970	PAUL WILLIAMS

We've only just begun, to live

White lace and promises

A kiss for luck and we're on our way

WE'VE ONLY JUST BEGUN	
1970	PAUL WILLIAMS

The Cars

I don't mind you coming here

And wastin' all my time

'Cause when you're standin' oh so near

I kind of lose my mind...

I needed someone to feed

I guess you're just what I needed

I needed someone to bleed

JUST WHAT I NEEDED	
1978	RIC OCASEK

57

⟶ 58

Gene Chandler

As I walk through this world

Nothing can stop the Duke of Earl

And you are my girl

And no one can hurt you...

'Cause I'm the Duke of Earl

DUKE OF EARL	
1961	**EARL EDWARDS, EUGENE DIXON, BERNICE WILLIAMS**

Harry Chapin

And she handed me 20 dollars for a two fifty fare

And said, "Harry, keep the change"

She walked away in silence

It's strange how you never know

But we'd both gotten what we'd asked for, such a long, long time ago

You see, she was gonna be an actress

And I was gonna learn to fly

She took off to find the footlights, I took off for the sky

And here she's acting happy, inside her handsome home

And me I'm flying in my taxi

Taking tips and gettin' stoned;

I go flyin' so high when I'm stoned

TAXI	
1972	**HARRY CHAPIN**

Well, my son turned ten just the other day

He said, "Thanks for the ball, Dad, c'mon, let's play

Can you teach me to throw?" I said, "Not today

I got a lot to do," he said "That's ok"

And he walked away but his smile never dimmed, it said

"I'm gonna be like him, yeah, you know I'm gonna be like him...."

And as he hung up the phone it occurred to me

He'd grown up just like me, my boy was just like me

CAT'S IN THE CRADLE	
1974	**HARRY CHAPIN, SANDRA CHAPIN**

Harry Chapin, rehearsing for a show
with his brother, Tom.

UPI/BETTMANN

I am the morning DJ at W.O.L.D.D.D....

The bright good-morning voice who's heard but never seen

Feeling all of forty five—going on fifteen

W.O.L.D.	
1974	**HARRY CHAPIN**

Ray Charles

Hit the road, Jack

And don't you come back no more

HIT THE ROAD, JACK	
1961	**PERCY MAYFIELD**

Chicago

Does anybody really know what time it is?

Does anybody really care?

DOES ANYBODY REALLY KNOW WHAT TIME IT IS	
1970	**ROBERT LAMM**

Feeling like I ought to sleep...

Searching for something to say

Waiting for the break of day

25 OR 6 TO 4	
1970	**ROBERT LAMM**

Chubby Checker

Let's twist again, like we did last summer

Come on let's twist again, like we did last year

LET'S TWIST AGAIN	
1961	KAL MANN

"The Twist" caused people apart. And they're still dancing all these years

Eric Clapton

Bell bottom blues you made me cry

I don't wanna lose this feeling...

Do you wanna see me crawl across the floor to you

BELL BOTTOM BLUES	
1970	ERIC CLAPTON

She took my hand, tried to make me understand

That she would always be there

But I looked Away

And she ran away from me today

I LOOKED AWAY	
1970	ERIC CLAPTON, BOBBY WHITLOCK

What'll you do when you get lonely

When nobody's waiting by your side?

You've been running and hiding much too long

You know it's just your foolish pride

Layla, you got me on my knees

LAYLA	
1970	ERIC CLAPTON, JIM GORDON

Eric Clapton.

Tell me who's been foolin' you?

Tell the Truth, who's been fooling who?...

The whole world is shakin' now, can you feel it?

TELL THE TRUTH	
1970	**ERIC CLAPTON, BOBBY WHITLOCK**

to dance apart later.

CHUBBY CHECKER

The rain is falling through the mist

Of sorrow that surrounded me

The sun could never melt away

The mist that may surround me

LET IT RAIN	
1972	**ERIC CLAPTON**

Standing at the crossroads, tryin' to read the signs

To tell me which way I should go

To find the answer and all the time I know

Plant your love and let it grow

LET IT GROW	
1974	**ERIC CLAPTON**

Lay down Sally, no need to leave so soon

I've been trying all night long just to talk to you

LAY DOWN SALLY	
1977	**ERIC CLAPTON, MARCY LEVY, GEORGE TERRY**

61

⟶ 62

Petula Clark

Just listen to the music of the traffic in the city

Linger on the sidewalk where the neon signs are pretty

DOWNTOWN	
1964	**TONY HATCH**

The Clash

London calling to the faraway towns

Now that war is declared—and battle come down

London calling to the underworld

Come out of the cupboard, all you boys and girls.

London calling to imitation zone

Forget it brother you can go it alone

London calling to the zombies of death

Quit holding out and draw another breath.

LONDON CALLING	
1979	**JOE STRUMMER, MICK JONES**

So alone I keep the wolves at bay

And there's only one thing I can say

You didn't stand by me, no not at all

You didn't stand by me, no way

TRAIN IN VAIN	
1979	**JOE STRUMMER, MICK JONES**

This is England, land of illegal dances

This is England, land of one thousand stances

THIS IS ENGLAND	
1985	**JOE STRUMMER AND BERNARD RHODES**

Jimmy Cliff

And then the harder they come

The harder they fall

One and all

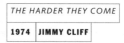

THE HARDER THEY COME	
1974	**JIMMY CLIFF**

The Coasters

Take out the papers and the trash

Or you don't get no spending cash

If you don't scrub that kitchen floor

You ain't gonna rock and roll no more

Yakety Yak, don't talk back...

You just put on your coat and hat

And walk yourself to the laundromat

And when you finish doing that

Bring in the dog and put out the cat

Yakety Yak, don't talk back

YAKETY YAK	
1958	JERRY LEIBER, MIKE STOLLER

He's gonna get caught, just you wait and see

Why's everybody always pickin' on me?

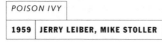

CHARLIE BROWN	
1959	JERRY LEIBER, MIKE STOLLER

She's pretty as a daisy

But look out man she's crazy

She'll really do you in

If you let her get under your skin

Poison ivy, poison ivy...

You're gonna need an ocean

Of calamine lotion

You'll be scratchin' like a hound

The minute you start to mess around

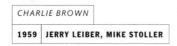

POISON IVY	
1959	JERRY LEIBER, MIKE STOLLER

Joe Cocker

Please don't ask me how many times I found you

Standing wet and naked in the garden

DELTA LADY	
1969	LEON RUSSELL

I've always done me little theatrical
throwing me arms about with the music.
think it's a bit too much. Like when I was
Sullivan, they surrounded me with
dancers to keep me

JOE COCKER

Leonard Cohen

Suzanne takes you down

to her place near the river

you can hear the boats go by

you can spend the night beside her

And you know that she's half crazy

but that's why you want to be there

and she feeds you tea and oranges

that come all the way from China

And just when you mean to tell her

that you have no love to give her

then she gets you on her wavelength

and she lets the river answer

that you've always been her lover...

And you want to travel with her

you want to travel blind

and you know that she can trust you

for you've touched her perfect body

With your mind

SUZANNE	
1966	**LEONARD COHEN**

A scheme is not a vision

and you never have been tempted

by a demon or a god...

When it all comes down to dust,

I will kill you if I must,

I'll help you if I can.

When it all comes down to dust,

lity bit of
Some people
on Ed
thousands of
hidden.

I will help you if I must,

I will kill you if I can.

And mercy on our uniform

man of peace, man of war—

the peacock spreads his fan!

I saw a beggar leaning on his wooden crutch

He said to me "You must not ask for so much"

And a pretty woman leaning in her darkened door

She cried to me "Hey, why not ask for more?"

I remember you well in the Chelsea Hotel

you were talking so brave and so sweet;

giving me head on the unmade bed...

while the limousines wait in the street.

And those were the reasons, and that was New York,

we were running for the money and the flesh:

and that was called love for the workers in song,

probably still is for those of them left...

But you got away, didn't you, baby,

you just turned your back on the crowd...

I remember you well in the Chelsea Hotel,

you were famous, your heart was a legend.

You told me again you preferred handsome men,

but for me you would make an exception.

And clenching your fist for the ones like us

who are oppressed by the figures of beauty,

you fixed yourself, you said: "Well, never mind,

we are ugly but we have the music."...

There is a war between the rich and poor,

a war between the man and the woman.

There is a war between the ones who say

"there is a war", and the ones who

say "there isn't"

THERE IS A WAR	
1974	LEONARD COHEN

Phil Collins

I can feel it coming in the air tonight, oh lord

I've been waiting for this moment for all my life

IN THE AIR TONIGHT	
1981	PHIL COLLINS

Commander Cody and the Lost Airmen

My daddy said "Son,

You're gonna drive me to drinkin'

If you don't stop drivin' that hot rod Lincoln"

HOT ROD LINCOLN	
1972	CHARLES RYAN, W.S. STEVENSON

Johnny Carson:

Arthur Conley

Do you like good music

That sweet soul music

SWEET SOUL MUSIC	
1967	OTIS REDDING, ARTHUR CONLEY, SAM COOKE

Sam Cooke

Cupid, please draw back your bow

And let your arrow go

Straight to my lover's heart for me

CUPID	
1961	SAM COOKE

Here's a man in evening clothes

How he got here I don't know

But man you oughta see him go

Twistin' the night away

TWISTIN' THE NIGHT AWAY	
1962	**SAM COOKE**

Instead of being my deliverance

She had a strange resemblance

To a cat name Frankenstein

ANOTHER SATURDAY NIGHT	
1963	**SAM COOKE**

So, why do they call you *Alice*?

Alice Cooper: It's a show, Johnny. Don't tell me you're like *this* in real life. • ON THE TONIGHT SHOW

Alice Cooper

I've got a baby's brain and an old man's heart

Took eighteen year to get this far

Don't always know what I'm talkin' about

Feels like I'm livin' in the middle of doubt

'Cause I'm eighteen, I get confused every day

Eighteen I just don't know what to say

Eighteen, I got to get away...

I'm in the middle, the middle of life

I'm a boy and I'm a man

I'm 18 and I like it

I'M EIGHTEEN	
1971	**ALICE COOPER, NEAL SMITH, MICHAEL BRUCE, GLEN BUXTON, DENNIS DUNAWAY**

We were upper middle class suburban brats that had anything we wanted. The whole end is that we are what we are now—a living social criticism. **ALICE COOPER**

Well we got no choice

All the girls and boys

Making all that noise

'Cause they found new toys

Well we can't salute ya

Can't find a flag

If that don't suit ya

That's a drag

School's out for summer

School's out forever...

We got no class, and we got no principles

SCHOOL'S OUT	
1972	ALICE COOPER, NEAL SMITH, MICHAEL BRUCE, GLEN BUXTON, DENNIS DUNAWAY

I got no friends 'cause they read the papers

They can't be seen, with me...

And I'm gettin' shot down and I'm, feelin' mean

No More Mister Nice Guy

No More Mister Clean...

They say he's sick and obscene

NO MORE MISTER NICE GUY	
1973	MICHAEL BRUCE AND ALICE COOPER

Just because I cut the heads off dolls, they say I must hate babies. But it's not true. I just hate dolls. ALICE COOPER

Elvis Costello

I'm not gonna get too sentimental

Like those other sticky valentines

ALISON	
1977	ELVIS COSTELLO

Music has to get to the people. In the heart, in the head, I don't care where, so long as it fucking gets them! ELVIS COSTELLO

⟶ 70

As I walk through this wicked world

Searching for light in the darkness of insanity

I ask myself, Is all hope lost?

Is there only pain and hatred and misery

And each time I feel like this inside

There's one thing I wanna know

What's so funny about peace, love, and understanding?...

'Cause each time I feel it slippin' away

It makes me wanna cry

What's so funny about peace, love, and understanding?

(WHAT'S SO FUNNY ABOUT) PEACE, LOVE AND UNDERSTANDING	
1978	**NICK LOWE**

It's the damage that we do we never know

It's the words that we don't say that scare me so

ACCIDENTS WILL HAPPEN	
1979	**ELVIS COSTELLO**

All it takes is one itchy trigger

One more widow or a less white nigger

OLIVER'S ARMY	
1979	**ELVIS COSTELLO**

You think I'm psycho, don't you mamma

I didn't mean to make you cry

PSYCHO	
1981	**LEON PAYNE**

Country Joe McDonald

Come on all you big strong men

Uncle Sam needs your help again

He's got himself in a terrible jam

Way down yonder in Viet Nam

So put down your books and pick up a gun

We're gonna have a whole lot of fun!

And it's one, two, three

What are we fighting for

Don't ask me, I don't give a damn

Next stop is Viet Nam

And it's five, six, seven

Open up the Pearly Gates

There ain't no time to wonder why

Whoopie, we're all gonna die!...

Come on, Wall Street, don't be slow

Why, man, this war is au-go-go

There's plenty good money to be made

Supplyin' the army with the tools of the trade

Just hope and pray if they drop the Bomb

They drop it on the Viet Cong!

Come on, mothers, throughout the land

Pack your boys off to Viet Nam

Come on, fathers, don't hesitate

Send your sons off before it's too late

Be the first one on your block

To have your boy come home in a box

FEEL LIKE I'M FIXIN' TO DIE RAG	
1969	**JOE MCDONALD**

Coven

Go ahead and hate your neighbor...

Do it in the name of Heaven

You can justify it in the end

ONE TIN SOLDIER (THE LEGEND OF BILLY JACK)	
1971	**DENNIS LAMBERT, BRIAN POTTER**

The Cowsills

Give me a head with hair

Long beautiful hair

Shining, gleaming streaming flaxen waxen

HAIR	
1966	**JAMES RADO, GEROME RAGNI**

71

⟶ 72

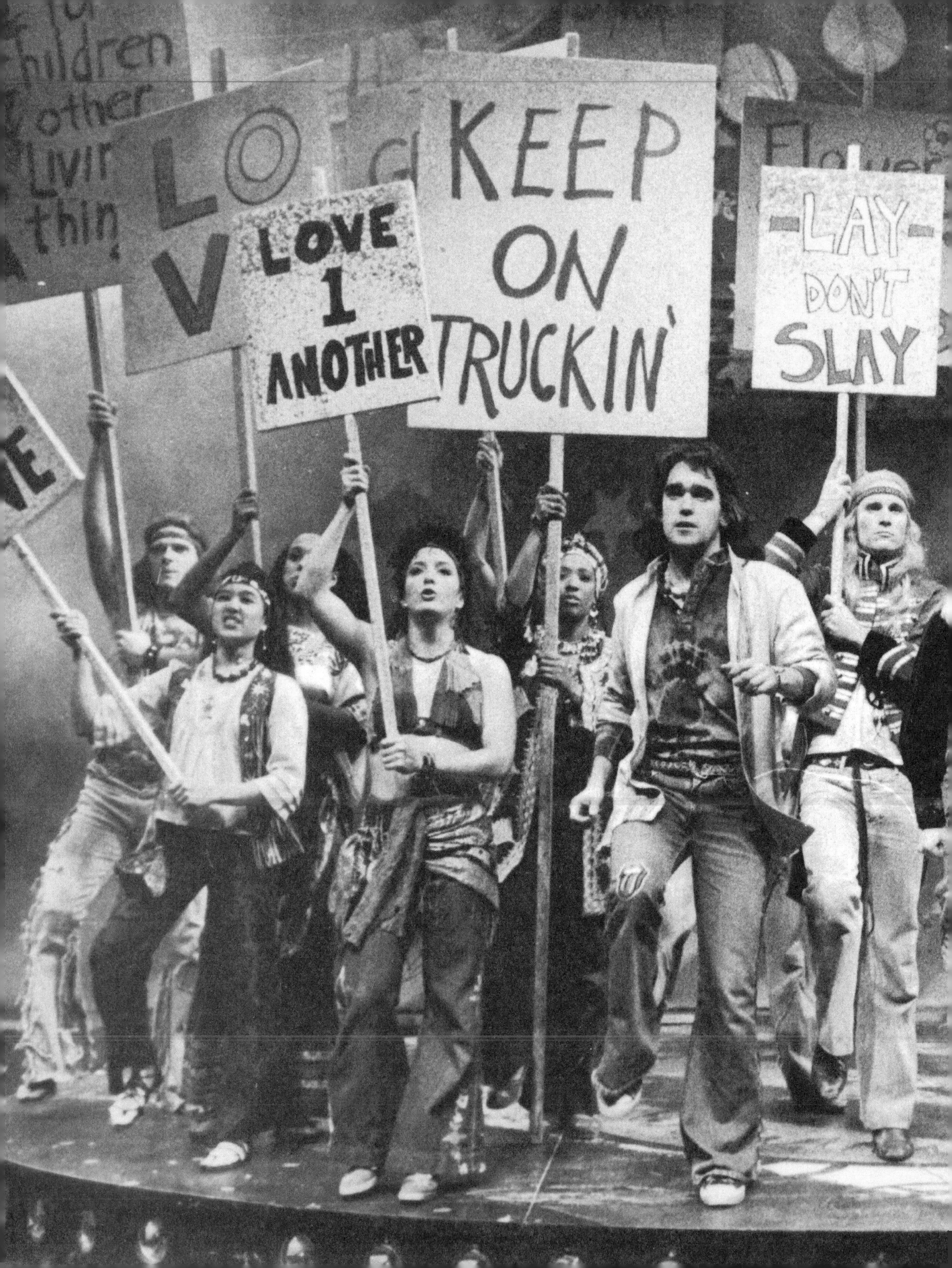
LOVE 1 ANOTHER
KEEP ON TRUCKIN'
-LAY- DON'T SLAY

The musical "Hair" opened on Broadway in 1968 and enjoyed a run of 1,750 performances.

Cream

I've been waiting so long

To be where I'm going

In the sunshine of your love

SUNSHINE OF YOUR LOVE	
1968	JACK BRUCE, PETER BROWN, ERIC CLAPTON

Tiny purple fishes run laughing through your fingers

And you want to take her with you

To the hard land of the winter

TALES OF BRAVE ULYSSES	
1968	ERIC CLAPTON, MARTIN SHARP

I'll wait in this place

Where the sun never shines…

Where the shadows run from themselves

WHITE ROOM	
1968	JACK BRUCE, PETER BROWN

Creedence Clearwater Revival

Left a good job in the city

Workin' for the man every night and day…

Cleaned alot of plates in Memphis

Pumped alot of pain in New Orleans

But I never saw the good side of the city

Until I hitched a ride on a river boat queen

Big wheel keep on turnin'

Proud Mary keep on burnin'

Rollin', rollin', rollin' on the river

PROUD MARY	
1968	JOHN FOGERTY

If a guy wants to wear his hair down
I'm not revolted by it. But I don't
and say, "Now there's a
like to spend next winter

Now when I was just a little boy…

My poppa said, "Son, don't let the man get you

And do what he done to me."

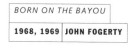

BORN ON THE BAYOU	
1968, 1969	JOHN FOGERTY

I fear rivers overflowing

I hear the voice of rage and ruin…

BAD MOON RISING	
1969	JOHN FOGERTY

You don't need a penny just to hang around

But if you've got a nickel, won't you lay you're money down!…

DOWN ON THE CORNER	
1969	JOHN FOGERTY

Some folks inherit star-spangled eyes…

And when you ask them, "How much should we give?"

They only answer More! More! More!

FORTUNATE SON	
1969	JOHN FOGERTY

Old Cody Junior took me over

Said, "You're gonna find the world is smoud'rin

If you get lost come on home to the Green River"

GREEN RIVER	
1969	JOHN FOGERTY

If I only had a dollar, for ev'ry song I've sung

And ev'ry time I had to play while people sat there drunk

You know I'd catch the next train back to where I live

Oh Lord! I'm stuck in Lodi again

LODI	
1969	JOHN FOGERTY

to his ass,
look at him
fella I'd
with." JOHN WAYNE

The devil's on the loose

Better run through the jungle...

Whoah, Don't look back

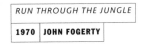

RUN THROUGH THE JUNGLE

1970	JOHN FOGERTY

Seven-thirty-seven comin' out of the sky

Won't you take me down to Memphis on a

Midnight ride, I wanna move

TRAVELIN' BAND

1970	JOHN FOGERTY

Long as I remember the rain been coming down

Clouds of mystery pouring

Confusion on the ground

Good men through the ages

Trying to find the sun

And I wonder, still wonder

Who'll stop the rain?

WHO'LL STOP THE RAIN

1970	JOHN FOGERTY

The Crest

Sixteen candles make a lovely light

But not as bright as your eyes tonight

SIXTEEN CANDLES

1958	LUTHER DIXON, ALLYSON R. KHENT

Crispian St. Peters

Come on baby, can't you see

I'm the Pied Piper, trust in me...

THE PIED PIPER

1966	ARTIE KORNFELD, STEVE DUBOFF

Jim Croce

Operator, could help me place this call

You see the number on the matchbook is old and faded...

Isn't that the way they say it goes

But let's forget all that

And give me the number if you can find it

So I can call just to tell them I'm fine

And to show I've overcome the blow

I've learned to take it well

I only wish my words could just convince myself

OPERATOR (THAT'S NOT THE WAY IT FEELS)	
1971, 1972	JIM CROCE

But there never seems to be enough time

To do the things you want to do once you find them

I've looked around enough to know

That you're the one I want to go thru time with

TIME IN A BOTTLE	
1971, 1972	JIM CROCE

And they say, "You don't tug on Superman's cape

You don't spit into the wind

You don't pull the mask off the Lone Ranger

And you don't mess around with Jim."

YOU DON'T MESS AROUND WITH JIM	
1971, 1972	JIM CROCE

77

Well, the Southside of Chicago

Is the baddest part of town

And if you go down there you better just beware

Of a man name of Leroy Brown...

And he's bad, bad Leroy Brown

Baddest man in the whole damned town

Badder than old King Kong

Meaner than a junkyard dog

BAD, BAD LEROY BROWN	
1972, 1973, 1986	JIM CROCE

So don't be getting excited when you hear that slammin' door

'Cause there'll be one less set of footsteps

On your floor in the mornin'

ONE LESS SET OF FOOTSTEPS	
1972, 1973	JIM CROCE

Yeah, I've had my share of broken dreams

And more than a couple of falls

And in chasin' what I thought were moonbeams

I have run into a couple of walls

THE HARD WAY EVERY TIME	
1973, 1974	JIM CROCE

Movin' me down the highway...

Movin' ahead so life won't pass me by

I GOT A NAME	
1973	NORMAN GIMBEL

So I'll hope that you can find another

Who can take what I could not...

Cause I never was much of a martyr before

And I ain't 'bout to start nothin' new

And baby, I can't hang upon no lover's cross for you

LOVER'S CROSS	
1973, 1974	**JIM CROCE**

You know a man of my ability

Should be smokin' on a big cigar

But till I get myself straight

I guess I'll just have to wait

In my rubber suit a-rubbin' these cars...

So baby, don't expect to see me

With no double martini

In any high brow society news

Cause I got them steadily depressin'

Low down mind messin'

Workin' at the carwash Blues

WORKIN' AT THE CARWASH BLUES	
1973, 1974	**JIM CROCE**

Crosby and Nash

Immigration Man

I won't toe your line today

I can't see it anyway

IMMIGRATION MAN	
1972, 1973	**DAVID CROSBY, GRAHAM NASH**

Crosby, Stills, Nash and Young

You know there's something that's going on here

That surely, surely won't stand the light of day

LONG TIME GONE	
1968	**DAVID CROSBY**

, Thank you, we needed that
we've ever played in front of

(the applause). This is the second time people, man. We're scared shitless.

STEPHEN STILLS, AT WOODSTOCK

Crosby, Stills, Nash and Young in Seattle, 1974. L\R: Stephen Stills, David Crosby, Graham Nash, Neil Young.

UPI/BETTMANN

He was tired of being poor

And he wasn't into selling door to door

4 & 20	
1969, 1971	STEPHEN STILLS

Forty nine reasons all in a line

All of them good ones, all of them lies

49 BYE-BYES	
1969	STEPHEN STILLS

Love isn't lying, it's loose in a lady who lingers

HELPLESSLY HOPING	
1969	STEPHEN STILLS

Ducks, and pigs, and chickens all

Animal carpets wall to wall

MARRAKESH EXPRESS	
1969	GRAHAM NASH

It's getting to the point where I'm no fun anymore

I am sorry...

SUITE: JUDY BLUE EYES	
1969	STEPHEN STILLS

Can you tell me please, who won?...

We are leaving, you don't need us

WOODEN SHIPS	
1969	DAVID CROSBY, STEPHEN STILLS, PAUL KANTNER

Are you thinkin' of telephones and managers

And where you got to be at noon?

YOU DON'T HAVE TO CRY	
1969	STEPHEN STILLS

Almost cut my hair...

But I didn't and I wonder why

I feel like letting my freak flag fly

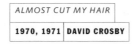

ALMOST CUT MY HAIR

1970, 1971 | **DAVID CROSBY**

If I had ever been here before

I would probably know just what to do

Don't you?

DEJA VU

1970, 1971 | **DAVID CROSBY**

Tin soldiers and Nixon coming

We're finally on our own...

Four dead in Ohio

OHIO

1970 | **NEIL YOUNG**

And you, of the tender years

Can't know the fears

That your elders grew by

TEACH YOUR CHILDREN

1970 | **GRAHAM NASH**

She has seen the changes

It ain't easy rearranging

SEE THE CHANGES

1977, 1978 | **STEPHEN STILLS**

So much time to make up

Everywhere you turn

Time we have wasted on the way

WASTED ON THE WAY

1982 | **GRAHAM NASH**

The Crystals

And he goes downtown

Where everybody's his boss

And he's lost in an angry land

UPTOWN	
1962	BARRY MANN, CYNTHIA WEIL

The Cyrkle

It's a turn down day

Nothing on my mind...

And I dig it

TURN DOWN DAY	
1966	JERRY KELLER, DAVID BLUME

Charlie Daniels Band

Every summer when it rains

I smell the jungle, I hear the planes

Can't tell no one, I feel ashamed

STILL IN SAIGON	
1981	DAN DALEY

Danny and the Juniors

Well, you can rock it, you can roll it

Do the slop and even stroll it at the hop

Where the jumpin' is the smoothest

And the music is the coolest, at the hop

AT THE HOP	
1957	ARTIE SINGER, JOHN MADARA, DAVID WHITE

Rock and roll is here to stay

And it will never die

It was meant to be that way

Though I don't know why

ROCK AND ROLL IS HERE TO STAY	
1958	DAVID WHITE

Bobby Darin

Splish splash I was takin' a bath...

Well, how was I to know there was a party going on?

SPLISH SPLASH	
1958	BOBBY DARIN, JEAN MURRAY

I want a dream lover

So I don't have to dream alone

DREAM LOVER	
1959	BOBBY DARIN

If I were a carpenter and you were a lady

Would you marry me anyway, would you have my baby?

IF I WERE A CARPENTER	
1966	TIM HARDIN

James Darren

Goodbye cruel world, I'm off to join the circus

Gonna be a broken-hearted clown...

Shoot me out of a cannon I don't care

Let the people point at me and stare...

That mean fickle woman

Made a cryin' clown of me

GOODBYE CRUEL WORLD	
1961	GLORIA SHAYNE

Bobby Day

He rocks in the tree top all day long

Hoppin' and a-boppin' and a-singin' his song...

The wise old owl, the big black crow

Flap their wings, singin' "Go bird, go"

ROCKIN' ROBIN	
1958	JIMMIE THOMAS

Deep Purple

We all came out to Montreaux on the Lake Geneva shoreline

To make records with the mobile, we didn't have much time.

Frank Zappa and the Mothers were at the best place around

But some stupid with a flare gun burned the place to the ground.

SMOKE ON THE WATER	
1972	RITCHIE BLACKMORE, IAN GILLAN, ROGER GLOVER, JON LORD, IAN PAICE

If it's too loud, you're too

TED NUGENT

John Denver

Now his life is full of wonder

But his heart still knows some fear

Of a simple thing he cannot comprehend

ROCKY MOUNTAIN HIGH	
1972	JOHN DENVER, MIKE TAYLOR

Aye Calypso, the places you've been to

The things that you've shown us, the stories you tell

Aye Calypso, I sing to your spirit

CALYPSO	
1975	JOHN DENVER

Neil Diamond

We got all night

To set the world right

We'll find us a dream that don't ask no questions

CRACKLIN' ROSIE	
1970	NEIL DIAMOND

But now days I'm lost between two shores

L.A.'s fine but it ain't home

New York's home, but it ain't mine no more

I AM... I SAID	
1971	NEIL DIAMOND

Bo Diddley

All you pretty women stand in line

I can make love to you

In a hour's time

I'm a man

I spell M. A. N. Man

I'M A MAN	
1955	**ELLAS MCDANIEL**

old.   They record the song and the white stations
start playing it. It's the same song, but they
call me "rhythm and blues" and they call the
white boy "rock 'n' roll". Just so long as it
was separate, they could make believe it wasn't
a black record anymore. But it
was written by a
black dude—me.
BO DIDDLEY

I walk forty seven miles of barb wire

Use a cobra snake for a necktie

Got a brand new house on the roadside

Made from rattlesnake hide

I got a brand new chimney made on top

Made from a human skull

Now come on baby let's take a little walk

And tell me, Who do you love?...

I got a tombstone hand a graveyard mine

I lived long enough

And I ain't scared o' dyin'

Who do you love?

WHO DO YOU LOVE?	
1956	**ELLAS MCDANIEL**

Mark Dinning

What was it you were looking for

That took your life that night...

Teen angel, can you hear me

TEEN ANGEL	
1969	**JEAN SURREY, RED SURREY**

> It was kinda like stuffing the wrong card in a computer, when you're, stickin' those artificial stimulants.
>
> **DION ON HIS HEROIN USE**

Dion

When I'm away, I wonder what you do

I wonder why I'm sure you're always true

I WONDER WHY	
1958	**RICARDO WEEKS, MELVIN ANDERSON**

Here's my story, it's sad but true

It's about a girl that I once knew

She took my love and ran around

RUNAROUND SUE	
1961	**DION DIMUCCI, ERNEST MARESCA**

I'm the type of guy that likes to roam around

I'm never in one place, I roam from town to town

THE WANDERER	
1961	**ERNEST MARESCA**

Has anybody here seen my old friend Martin,

Can you tell me where he's gone?

He freed a lotta people

But it seems the good die young

But I looked around and he's gone...

Has anybody here seen my old friend Bobby,

Can you tell me where he's gone?

I thought I saw him walkin' up over the hill—

With Abraham, Martin, and John

ABRAHAM, MARTIN AND JOHN	
1968	**RICHARD L. HOLLER**

Dire Straits

And Harry doesn't mind if he doesn't make the scene

He's got a daytime job, he's doin' alright

SULTANS OF SWING	
1978	**MARK KNOPFLER**

Willie Dixon

I am a back door man

Well, the men don't know

But the little girls understand

BACK DOOR MAN	
1965	WILLIE DIXON

Dr. Hook and the Medicine Show

We sing about beauty and we sing about truth

At ten thousand dollars a show

COVER OF "ROLLING STONE"	
1973	SHEL SIVERSTEIN

Fats Domino

You made me cry when you said goodbye

Ain't that a shame!

AIN'T THAT A SHAME	
1955	ANTOINE "FATS" DOMINO, DAVE BARTHOLOMEW

I found my thrill

On Blueberry Hill

BLUEBERRY HILL	
1956	AL LEWIS, LARRY STOCK, VINCENT ROSE

Sunday mornin' my head is so bad

But it's worth it for the times I've had

BLUE MONDAY	
1957	FATS DOMINO AND DAVE BARTHOLOMEW

I'm walkin', yes indeed and I'm talkin'...

What'ya gonna do when the well runs dry?

I'M WALKIN'	
1957	ANTOINE "FATS" DOMINO, DAVE BARTHOLOMEW

Donovan

In the chilly hours and minutes of uncertainty
I want to be in the warm hold of your loving mind
To feel you all around me, and to take your hand along the sand
Ah, but I may as well try and catch the wind

CATCH THE WIND	
1965	DONOVAN LEITCH

He's five feet two and he's six feet four
He fights with missiles and with spears

UNIVERSAL SOLDIER	
1965	BUFFY SAINTE-MARIE

Townsperson:

Electrical bananas is gonna be a sudden craze
Electrical banana is bound to be the very next phase
They call me Mellow Yellow (quite rightly)

MELLOW YELLOW	
1966	DONOVAN LEITCH

When I look out my window
Many sights to see
And when I look in my window
So many different people to be
That it's strange, so strange
Must be the season of the witch

SEASON OF THE WITCH	
1966	DONOVAN LEITCH

Sunshine came softly through my window today
Could've tripped out easy, but I've changed my ways...
Any trick in the book, now baby that I find
Superman or Green Lantern ain't got a-nothin' on me

SUNSHINE SUPERMAN	
1966	DONOVAN LEITCH

Donovan, the Scottish troubadour and songwriter, 1969.

THE BETTMANN ARCHIVE

Doobie Brothers

You don't know me but I'm your brother

I was raised here in this living hell

You don't know my kind in your world

Fairly soon, time will tell

You, telling me the things you're gonna do for me

I've found that I didn't like what I think I see

Takin' it to the streets

TAKIN' IT TO THE STREETS	
1972	**MICHAEL MCDONALD**

What are you rebelling against?
Marlon Brando: Whadda ya got?

FROM THE 1955 FILM, **THE WILD ONE**

And though it's a part of the Lone Star State

People don't seem to care

They just keep on looking to the East

CHINA GROVE	
1973	**TOM JOHNSTON**

Down around the corner a half a mile from here

You see them old trains runnin' and you watch them disappear

Without love, where would you be now?

You know I saw Miss Lucy down along the tracks;

She lost her home and family and she won't be comin' back

Without love, where would you be now?

LONG TRAIN RUNNIN'	
1973	**TOM JOHNSTON**

South City midnight lady, I'm much obliged indeed

You sure have saved this man whose soul was in need

I thought there was no reason for all these things I do

But the smile that I sent out returned with you

SOUTH CITY MIDNIGHT LADY	
1973	**PATRICK SIMMONS**

Oh black water, keep on rolling

Mississippi Moon won't you keep on shining on me

Just keep on shining your light

BLACK WATER	
1974	**PAT SIMMONS**

The Doors

Tried to run, tried to hide

Break on through to the other side

BREAK ON THROUGH	
1966	**JIM MORRISON, JOHN DENSMORE, ROBERT KRIEGER, RAYMOND MANZAREK**

Turn me out and I'll wander baby

Stumblin' in the neon groves

SOUL KITCHEN	
1966	**JIM MORRISON, JOHN DENSMORE, ROBERT KRIEGER, RAYMOND MANZAREK**

Well she's fashionably lean

And she's fashionably late

TWENTIETH CENTURY FOX	
1966	**JIM MORRISON, JOHN DENSMORE, ROBERT KRIEGER, RAYMOND MANZAREK**

Show me the way to the next whiskey bar

Oh, don't ask why, oh don't ask why

ALABAMA SONG (THE WHISKEY BAR)	
1967	**KURT WEILL**

Before you slip into unconsciousness

I'd like to have another kiss

THE CRYSTAL SHIP	
1967	**JIM MORRISON, JOHN DENSMORE, ROBERT KRIEGER, RAYMOND MANZAREK**

Morrison never struck me as an
authentic rock and roller. There was
not enough joy in his music.
ALEC DUNBRO

The Doors at a London press conference in 1968. L\R: John Densmore, Ray Manzarek, Jim Morrison, and Robby Krieger.

UPI/BETTMANN

Jim Morrison in concert.

©Don Paulsen/MICHAEL OCHS ARCHIVES

This is the end
My only friend, the end

THE END	
1967	**JIM MORRISON, JOHN DENSMORE, ROBERT KRIEGER, RAYMOND MANZAREK**

The time to hesitate is through...
Come on baby light my fire
Try to set the night on fire

LIGHT MY FIRE	
1967	**ROBERT KRIEGER**

Love me two times girl
One for tomorrow, one just for today

LOVE ME TWO TIMES	
1967	**ROBERT KRIEGER**

People are strange when you're a stranger
Faces look ugly when you're alone

PEOPLE ARE STRANGE	
1967	**JIM MORRISON, JOHN DENSMORE, ROBERT KRIEGER, RAYMOND MANZAREK**

Five to one, baby, one in five
No one here gets out alive

FIVE TO ONE	
1968	**JIM MORRISON, JOHN DENSMORE, ROBERT KRIEGER, RAYMOND MANZAREK**

Hello, I love you, won't you tell me your name?

HELLO, I LOVE YOU	
1968	**JIM MORRISON, JOHN DENSMORE, ROBERT KRIEGER, RAYMOND MANZAREK**

C'mon, c'mon, c'mon, c'mon now touch me babe
Can't you see that I am not afraid

TOUCH ME	
1969	**JIM MORRISON, JOHN DENSMORE, ROBERT KRIEGER, RAYMOND MANZAREK**

You like people? I hate 'em... screw 'em... I don't need 'em... Oh, I need 'em... to grow potatoes.

JIM MORRISON

93

⟶ 94

Are you a lucky little lady in the city of light?

Or just another lost angel—city of night

L.A. WOMAN	
1971	**JIM MORRISON, JOHN DENSMORE, ROBERT KRIEGER, RAYMOND MANZAREK**

Don't you love her

As she's walkin' out the door

LOVE HER MADLY	
1971	**JIM MORRISON, JOHN DENSMORE, ROBERT KRIEGER, RAYMOND MANZAREK**

Lee Dorsey

Working in the coal mine

Goin' down, down, down...

Whoops, about to slip dow-ow-wn

WORKING IN THE COAL MINE	
1966	**ALLEN TOUSSAINT**

The Drifters

But don't forget who's taking you home

And in whose arms you're gonna be

So darling, save the last dance for me

SAVE THE LAST DANCE FOR ME	
1960	**DOC POMUS, MORT SHUMAN**

This magic moment, so different and so new

Was like any other until I met you

THIS MAGIC MOMENT	
1960	**DOC POMUS, MORT SHUMAN**

They say the neon lights are bright on Broadway

They say there's always magic in the air

ON BROADWAY	
1963	**CYNTHIA WEILL, BARRY MANN, JERRY LEIBER, MIKE STOLLER**

Gerry Goffin and Carole King, at the RCA recording studio in 1959. These two, once married, were members of Don Kirshner's legendary Brill Building songwriters. Others included Neil Sedaka, Cynthia Weil, Barry Mann, Howard Greenfield, Bobby Darin, and Neil Diamond.

MICHAEL OCHS ARCHIVES

I keep on telling you

Right smack dab in the middle of town

I've found a paradise that's trouble proof

UP ON THE ROOF	
1963	**GERRY GOFFIN AND CAROLE KING**

The Kirshner years were really good for about a year. And then I started thinking, Am I gonna write this shit until I'm thirty-two? I keep thinking that God is going to get my ass any minute because this isn't a fit occupation for a man.
GERRY GOFFIN

Under the boardwalk, out of the sun

Under the boardwalk, we'll be havin' some fun

Under the boardwalk, people walkin' above

Under the boardwalk, we'll be making love

UNDER THE BOARDWALK	
1964	**ARTHUR RESNICK, KENNY YOUNG**

Ian Dury and the Blockheads

Sex and drugs and rock and roll

Is all my brain and body need...

Is very good indeed

SEX & DRUGS & ROCK 'N' ROLL	
1977	**IAN DURY, C. JANKEL**

Bob Dylan

Yes, 'n' how many years can some people exist

Before they're allowed to be free?

Yes, 'n' how many times can a man turn his head

Pretending he just doesn't see?

The answer, my friend, is blowin' in the wind

The answer is blowin' in the wind

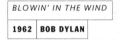

BLOWIN' IN THE WIND

1962 | BOB DYLAN

So I'll just say fare thee well

I ain't sayin' you treated me unkind

You could have done better but I don't mind

You just kinda wasted my precious time

But don't think twice, it's all right

DON'T THINK TWICE IT'S ALRIGHT

1963 | BOB DYLAN

Oh, what did you see, my blue-eyed son?

Oh, what did you see, my darling young one?

I saw a white ladder all covered with water

I saw ten thousand talkers whose tongues were all broken

I saw guns and sharp swords in the hands of young children

And it's a hard, and it's a hard, it's a hard, it's a hard

And it's a hard rain's a-gonna fall

A HARD RAIN'S A GONNA FALL

1963 | BOB DYLAN

Come writers and critics who prophesize with your pens

And keep your eyes wide, the chance won't come again

And don't speak too soon for the wheel's still in spin

And there's no tellin' who that it's namin'

For the loser now will be later to win

For the times they are a-changin'

THE TIMES THEY ARE A-CHANGIN'

1963, 1964 | BOB DYLAN

Go'way from my window

Leave at your own chosen speed

I'm not the one you want, babe

I'm not the one you need...

Go melt back into the night babe

Everything inside is made of stone

There's nothing in here moving

An' anyway I'm not alone

You say you're looking for someone

Who'll pick you up each time you fall

To gather flowers constantly

An' to come each time you call

A lover for your life an' nothing more

But it ain't me, babe

No, no, no, it ain't me, babe

IT AIN'T ME BABE	
1964	**BOB DYLAN**

Nobody sings Dylan like Dylan.

A CBS RECORDS AD

Hey! Mr. Tambourine Man, play a song for me

I'm not sleepy and there is no place I'm going to

Hey! Mr. Tambourine Man, play a song for me

In the jingle jangle morning I'll come followin' you...

Yes, to dance beneath the diamond sky

With one hand waving free

Silhouetted by the sea

Circled by the circus sands

With all memory and fate

Driven deep beneath the waves

Let me forget about today until tomorrow

MR. TAMBOURINE MAN	
1964, 1965	**BOB DYLAN**

97

⟶ 98

Everything happened so qu[ick...] electricity in the air. I didn't ever want to go to s[leep...] miss anything. It wasn't t[...] there now. If you want to b[... suc-]cessful, you'll go and fin[d...]

BOB DYLAN

George Harrison organize[d...] at Madison Square Garde[n...] aid refugees from East Pa[kistan...] L\R: Ringo Starr, George [...] Leon Russell.

the 60's. There was just an
hard to explain.,I mean, you
because you didn't want,to
in the 70's and it ain't
artist and not just be suc-
electricity. It's somewhere.

Something is happening here

But you don't know what it is

Do you, Mister Jones

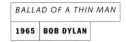

BALLAD OF A THIN MAN

1965 | BOB DYLAN

Oh God said to Abraham, "Kill me a son"

Abe says, "Man, you must be puttin' me on"

God say, "No." Abe say, "What?"

God say, "You can do what you want Abe, but

The next time you see me comin' you better run"

Well Abe says, "Where do you want this killin' done?"

God says, "Out on Highway 61."

HIGHWAY 61 REVISITED

1965 | BOB DYLAN

The hollow horn plays wasted words

Proves to warn

That he not busy being born

Is busy dying...

Temptation's page flies out the door

You follow, find yourself at war

Watch waterfalls of pity roar

You feel to moan but unlike before

You discover

That you'd just be

One more person crying...

Disillusioned words like bullets bark

As human gods aim for their mark

Made everything from toy guns that spark

To flesh-colored Christs that glow in the dark

It's easy to see without looking too far

That not much is really sacred...

Advertising signs that con you

Into thinking you're the one

That can do what's never been done

That can win what's never been won

Meantime life outside goes on

All around you...

Although the masters make the rules

For the wise man and the fools

I got nothing Ma, to live up to

IT'S ALRIGHT, MA (I'M ONLY BLEEDING)

1965 | **BOB DYLAN**

Once upon a time you dressed so fine

You threw the bums a dime in your prime, didn't you?...

You said you'd never compromise

With the mystery tramp, but now you realize

He's not selling any alibis

As you stare into the vacuum of his eyes

And ask him do you want to make a deal?

How does it feel, how does it feel

To be on your own with no direction home

Like a rolling stone

LIKE A ROLLING STONE

1965 | **BOB DYLAN**

I ain't gonna work on Maggie's farm no more

No, I ain't gonna work on Maggie's farm no more

Well, I wake in the morning

Fold my hands and pray for rain

I got a head full of ideas

That are drivin' me insane

It's a shame the way she makes me scrub the floor

I ain't gonna work on Maggie's farm no more

MAGGIE'S FARM

1965 | **BOB DYLAN**

I know the reason

That you talk behind my back

I used to be among the crowd

You're in with

Do you take me for such a fool

To think I'd make contact

With the one who tries to hide

What he don't know to begin with

POSITIVELY 4TH STREET

1965 | BOB DYLAN

Johnny's in the basement

Mixing up the medicine

I'm on the pavement

Thinking about the government...

Look out kid

It's somethin' you did

God knows when

But you're doin' it again

SUBTERRANEAN HOMESICK BLUES

1965 | BOB DYLAN

People call you this or that. But I can't respond,
seems like I'm defensive, and,
what does it matter, really?

BOB DYLAN, ON HIS EVER-CHANGING MUSICAL STYLES

She takes just like a woman

She makes love just like a woman

And she aches just like a woman

But she breaks like a little girl

JUST LIKE A WOMAN

1966 | BOB DYLAN

"There must be some way out of here," said the joker to the thief

"There's too much confusion, I can't get no relief"

"No reason to get excited," the thief, he kindly spoke

"There are many here among us who feel that life is but a joke"

ALL ALONG THE WATCHTOWER	
1968	**BOB DYLAN**

Lay, lady, lay, lay across my big brass bed

Stay, lady, stay, stay with your man awhile

Until the break of day, let me see you make him smile

LAY, LADY, LAY	
1969	**BOB DYLAN**

May your hands always be busy

May your feet always be swift

May you have a strong foundation

When the winds of changes shift.

May your heart always be joyful,

May your song always be sung,

May you stay forever young,

Forever young, forever young

May you stay forever young.

FOREVER YOUNG	
1973, 1974	**BOB DYLAN**

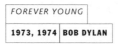
because then it
you know,

Mama, take this badge off of me

I can't use it anymore

It's gettin' dark, too dark for me to see

I feel like I'm knockin' on heaven's door

KNOCKIN' ON HEAVEN'S DOOR	
1973, 1974	**BOB DYLAN**

Sundown, yellow moon, I replay the past
I know every scene by heart, they all went by so fast
If she's passin' back this way, I'm not that hard to find
Tell her she can look me up if she's got the time

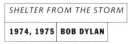

IF YOU SEE HER SAY HELLO

1974, 1975 | BOB DYLAN

Not a word was spoke between us, there was little risk involved
Everything up to that point had been left unresolved
Try imagining a place where it's always safe and warm
"Come in," she said
"I'll give you shelter from the storm."...
Now there's a wall between us, somethin' there's been lost
I took too much for granted, got my signals crossed
Just to think that it all began on a long-forgotten morn
"Come in," she said
"I'll give you shelter from the storm."

SHELTER FROM THE STORM

1974, 1975 | BOB DYLAN

He hears the ticking of the clocks
And walks along with a parrot that talks
Hunts her down by the waterfront docks where the sailors all come in
Maybe she'll pick him out again, how long must he wait
Once more for a simple twist of fate

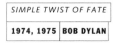

SIMPLE TWIST OF FATE

1974, 1975 | BOB DYLAN

She was workin' in a topless place
And I stopped in for a beer
I just kept lookin' at the side of her face

In the spotlight so clear

And later on as the crowd thinned out

I's just about to do the same

She was standing there in back of my chair

Said to me, "Don't I know your name?"

I muttered somethin' underneath my breath

She studied the lines on my face

I must admit I felt a little uneasy

When she bent down to tie the laces of my shoe

Tangled up in blue

TANGLED UP IN BLUE	
1974, 1975	BOB DYLAN

Time is an ocean, But it ends at the shore

OH SISTER	
1975, 1976	BOB DYLAN, JACQUES LEVY

You may be an ambassador to England or France,

You may like to gamble, you might like to dance,

You may be the heavyweight champion of the world,

You may be a socialite with a long string of pearls

But you're gonna have to serve somebody, yes indeed

You're gonna have to serve somebody,

Well, it may be the devil or it may be the Lord

But you're gonna have to serve somebody

GOTTA SERVE SOMBODY	
1979	BOB DYLAN

Standing on the waters casting your bread

While the eyes of the idol with the iron head are glowing.

Distant ships sailing into the mist,

You were born with a snake in both of your fists while a hurricane was blowing.

Freedom just around the corner for you

But with the truth so far off, what good will it do?...

Jokerman dance to the nightingale tune,

Bird fly high by the light of the moon,

Oh, oh, oh, Jokerman.

JOKERMAN	
1983	**BOB DYLAN**

Broken cutters, broken saws,

Broken buckles, broken laws,

Broken bodies, broken bones,

Broken voices on broken phones.

Take a deep breath, feel like you're chokin',

Everything is broken.

EVERYTHING IS BROKEN	
1989	**BOB DYLAN**

The Eagles

Lookin' for a lover

Who won't blow my cover

She's so hard to find

TAKE IT EASY	
1972	**JACKSON BROWNE, GLENN FREY**

Desperado, oh, you ain't gettin' no younger

your pain and your hunger, they're drivin' you home

And freedom, oh, freedom, well, that's just some people talkin'

Your prison is walkin' through this world all alone

Don't your feet get cold in the winter time?

The sky won't snow and the sun won't shine

It's hard to tell the night time from the day

You're losin' all your highs and lows

Ain't it funny how the feelin' goes away?

DESPERADO	
1973	**DON HENLEY, GLENN FREY**

Your twisted fate has found you out

And it's finally turned the tables

Stole your dreams and paid you with regret

Desperado.

You sealed your fate a long time ago

(Ain't it hard when you're all alone In the center ring)

Now there's no time left to borrow

Maybe tomorrow

DESPERADO PART II

1973 | DON HENLEY AND GLENN FREY

"All you bloodthirsty bystanders, will you try to find your seats?"

DOOLIN-DALTON PART II	
1973	**GLENN FREY, JOHN DAVID SOUTHER, DON HENLEY, JACKSON BROWNE**

Oh, and it's a hollow feelin'

When it comes down to dealin' friends

It never ends

Take another shot of courage

Wonder why the right words never come

You just get numb

It's another tequila sunrise

This old world still looks the same

Another frame

TEQUILA SUNRISE	
1973	**DON HENLEY, GLENN FREY**

Same dances in the same shoes

Same habits that you just can't lose;

There's no telling what a man might use

After the thrill is gone

The flame rises but it soon descends

Empty pages and a frozen pen;

You're not quite lovers and you're not quite friends

After the thrill is gone…

What can you do when your dreams come true

And it's not quite like you planned?…

Time passes and you must move on

Half the distance takes you twice as long;

So you keep on singing for the sake of the song

After the thrill is gone…

Any kind of love without passion

That ain't no kind of love at all

AFTER THE THRILL IS GONE	
1975	**DON HENLEY, GLENN FREY**

The Eagles, one version.

L\R: Don Henley, Joe Walsh,

Randy Meisner, Glenn Frey,

and Don Felder.

AP/WIDE WORLD PHOTOS

109

⟶ 110

City girls just seem to find out early

How to open doors with just a smile...

Late at night a big old house gets lonely;

I guess ev'ry form of refuge has its price...

She gets up and pours herself a strong one

And stares out at the stars up in the sky

Another night, it's gonna be a long one;

She draws the shade and hangs her head to cry

She wonders how it ever got this crazy;

She thinks about a boy she knew in school

Did she get tired or did she just get lazy?

She's so far gone she feels just like a fool...

You can't hide your lyin' eyes

And your smile is thin disguise

LYIN' EYES	
1975	**DON HENLEY, GLENN FREY**

I've been searching for the daughter of the devil himself;

I've been searching for an angel in white

I've been waiting for a woman who's a little of both

And I can feel her but she's nowhere in sight

Oo, loneliness will blind you in between the wrong and right

ONE OF THESE NIGHTS	
1975	**DON HENLEY, GLENN FREY**

On a dark desert highway

Cool wind in my hair

Warm smell of colitas

Rising up from the air

Up ahead in the distance

I saw a shimmering light

My head grew heavy and my sight grew dim

I had to stop for the night

There she stood in the doorway;

I heard the mission bell

Let them
Washington,
going to
Holly

And I was thinkin' to myself

This could be Heaven or this could be Hell...

There were voices down the corridor

I thought I heard them say

Welcome to the Hotel California

Such a lovely place

Such a lovely face

Plenty of room at the Hotel California

Any time of year

You can find it here

Her mind is Tiffany-twisted

She got the Mercedes bends

She got a lot of pretty, pretty boys

That she calls friends

How they dance in the courtyard

Sweet summer sweat

Some dance to remember

Some dance to forget...

Mirrors on the ceiling

Pink champagne on ice

And she said, We are all just prisoners here

Of our own device

And in the master's chambers

They gathered for a big feast

They stab it with their steely knives

But they just can't kill the beast

Last thing I remember

I was running for the door...

"Relax," said the night man

"We are programmed to receive

You can check out any time you like

But you can never leave"

HOTEL CALIFORNIA	
1976	DON HENLEY, GLENN FREY, AND DON FELDER

have
D.C. We're
take over
wood.

ABBIE HOFFMAN

111

They came from everywhere

To the Great Divide

Seeking a place to stand

Or a place to hide...

They called it Paradise

I don't know why

Somebody laid the mountains low

While the town got high...

We satisfy our endless needs

And justify our bloody deeds

In the name of Destiny

And in the name of God...

They call it Paradise

I don't know why

You call some place Paradise

Kiss it good-bye

THE LAST RESORT

1976	DON HENLEY AND GLENN FREY

He was a hard-headed man

He was brutally handsome

And she was terminally pretty...

They had one thing in common

They were good in bed

She say, "Faster, faster

The lights are turnin' red"

Life in the fast lane

Surely make you lose your mind...

They knew all the right people

They took all the right pills...

There were lines on the mirror

Lines on her face

She pretended not to notice

She was caught up in the race

Out ev'ry evenin'

Until it was light

He was too tired to make it

She was too tired to fight about it...

They went rushin' down that freeway

Messed around and got lost

They didn't know

They were just dyin' to get off

LIFE IN THE FAST LANE	
1976	**DON HENLEY, GLENN FREY, AND JOE WALSH**

You never thought you'd be alone

This far down the line

And I know what's been on your mind

You're afraid it's all been wasted time

So you live from day to day

And you dream about tomorrow

Oh, and the hours go like minutes

And the shadows come to stay

So ya take a little somethin'

To make them go away...

So you can get on with your search, baby

And I can get on with mine

And maybe someday we will find

That it wasn't really wasted time

WASTED TIME	
1976	**DON HENLEY AND GLENN FREY**

Edison Lighthouse

She's really got a magical spell

And it's working so well

That I can't get away

LOVE GROWS (WHERE MY ROSEMARY GOES)	
1970	**TONY MACAULAY, BARRY MASON**

Dave Edmunds

I begged you not to go, but you said goodbye

I hear you knockin' (but you can't come in)

I HEAR YOU KNOCKIN'	
1971	DAVE BARTHOLOMEW, PEARL KING

Electric Prunes

I had too much to dream last night

I'm not ready to face the light

I HAD TOO MUCH TO DREAM (LAST NIGHT)	
1966	NANCIE MANTZ, ANNETTE TUCKER

Emerson, Lake & Palmer

Let me tell you something

You just couldn't be more wrong

You see I really have to tell you

That it all gets so intense

From my experience

It just doesn't seem to make sense

Still you turn me on

STILL... YOU TURN ME ON	
1973	GREG LAKE

There might have been things I missed...

You see it's all clear

You were meant to be here

From the beginning

FROM THE BEGINNING	
1971	GREG LAKE

David Essex

Still lookin' for that blue jean, baby queen

Prettiest girl I've ever seen...

ROCK ON	
1973	DAVID ESSEX

Betty Everett

Is it in his eyes?

Oh no you'll be deceived

Is it in his heart?

Oh no he'll make believe

If you want to know if he loves you so

It's in his kiss

SHOOP SHOOP SONG	
1964	**RUDY CLARK**

The Everly Brothers

Bye bye love, bye bye happiness

Hello loneliness, I think I'm gonna cry

BYE BYE LOVE	
1957	**FELICE AND BOUDLEAUX BRYANT**

The movie's over it's four o'clock

And we're in trouble deep

Wake up little Susie

WAKE UP LITTLE SUSIE	
1957	**FELICE AND BOUDLEAUX BRYANT**

Only trouble is, gee whiz

I'm dreaming my life away

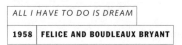

ALL I HAVE TO DO IS DREAM	
1958	**FELICE AND BOUDLEAUX BRYANT**

I die each time I hear this sound

Here he comes—that's Cathy's clown

CATHY'S CLOWN	
1960	**DON EVERLY, PHIL EVERLY**

The Fireballs

Bottle of wine, fruit of the vine

When you gonna let me get sober

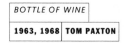

BOTTLE OF WINE	
1963, 1968	TOM PAXTON

First Class

Beach baby, beach baby lend me your hand

Give me something that I can remember

BEACH BABY	
1974	GILLIAN SHAKESPEARE

The First Edition

I just dropped in

To see what condition my condition was in

JUST DROPPED IN (TO SEE WHAT CONDITION MY CONDITION WAS IN)	
1968	M. NEWBURY

Five Man Electrical Band

Signs, signs, everywhere are signs

Blockin' up the scenery and breaking my mind

Do this, don't do that, can't you read the signs?

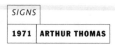

SIGNS	
1971	ARTHUR THOMAS

The Flamingos

Are the stars out tonight?

I don't know if it's cloudy or bright

I ONLY HAVE EYES FOR YOU	
1959	AL DUBIN

Fleetwood Mac

Getting back to the way I feel

Her honest word is my only real friend...

She's still a mystery to me

EMERALD EYES

1973 | **BOB WELCH**

Because there's no explaining what your imagination

Can make you see or feel

Seems like a dream, got me hypnotized

HYPNOTIZED

1973 | **BOB WELCH**

Fleetwood Mac, at their hit-producing peak.

L\R: John McVie, Christine McVie, Stevie Nicks, Mick Fleetwood, Lindsey Buckingham. UPI/BETTMANN

⟶ 118

I guess you heard about the Bermuda Triangle

There's something going on

Nobody seems to know just what it is

And the Air Force won't let on

Might be a hole down in the ocean

Yeah, or a fog that won't let go

Might be some crazy people talking

Or somebody that we ought to know

Down in Bermuda

Pale blue sea

Down in the Triangle

It's easy to believe

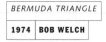

BERMUDA TRIANGLE

1974 | BOB WELCH

So when you get the feeling

The man you got's no good

Well just remember, heroes are so hard to find

HEROES ARE HARD TO FIND

1974 | CHRISTINE MCVIE

She came in like a hurricane. Wearing boots and diamond rings

With a fox-fur on her shoulder. She sent me wondering

And I could tell she was feeling abandoned

Because she flashed a couple looks my way

She said, "Hi four eyes, ya never asked me

But I'll tell ya anyway"

She took me out of the blackboard jungle

And put me straight in a hurricane

She hypnotized my eyes with her silver-heeled ways

If I could sing like Paul McCartney

And get hungry like Etta James

I'd never change, her silver-heeled ways

SILVER HEELS

1974 | BOB WELCH

Don't stop thinking about tomorrow

Don't stop, it'll soon be here

It'll be better than before

Yesterday's gone, yesterday's gone

DON'T STOP

1976 | **CHRISTINE MCVIE**

Loving you isn't the right thing to do

How can I ever change things that I feel...

You can go your own way

GO YOUR OWN WAY

1976 | **LINDSEY BUCKINGHAM**

You can take me to paradise

And then again you can be cold as ice

Think I'm lookin' on the dark side

But ev'ry day you hurt my pride

I'm over my head, but it sure feels nice...

Sometimes I can't help but feel

That I'm wasting all of my time

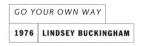

OVER MY HEAD

1976 | **CHRISTINE MCVIE**

Have mercy baby on a poor girl like me

You know I'm fallin', fallin', at your feet

I'm tingling right from my head to my toes

So help me, help me, help me make the feeling go

'Cause when the lovin' starts and the lights go down

There's not another living soul around

You woo me until the sun comes up

And you say that you love me...

Fallin', fallin', fallin'

SAY YOU LOVE ME

1976 | **CHRISTINE MCVIE**

I never did believe in miracles

But I've a feeling it's time to try

I never did believe in the ways of magic

But I'm beginning to wonder why

YOU MAKE LOVING FUN	
1976	CHRISTINE MCVIE

Run in the shadows, damn your love, damn your lies.!

I can still hear you saying you would never break the chain

THE CHAIN	
1977	LINDSEY BUCKINGHAM, CHRISTINE MCVIE, STEVIE NICKS,
	MICK FLEETWOOD, JOHN MCVIE

Eddie Floyd

The way you love me is fright'nin'

Everybody knock, knock, knock—on wood

KNOCK ON WOOD	
1966	EDDIE FLOYD, STEVE CROPPER

Dan Fogelberg

We drank a toast to innocence

We drank a toast to now...

SAME OLD LANG SYNE	
1980	DAN FOGELBERG

Foreigner

I was inside, looking outside

A million of faces and still I'm alone...

I'm looking out for the two of us

I hope we'll be here when they're through with us

LONG, LONG WAY FROM HOME	
1977	LOU GRAMMATICO

That's why I'm, hot blooded

Shake it and see

I got a fever of a hundred and three

C'mon baby do you do more than dance...

Shall I leave you my key

HOT BLOODED	
1978	**LOU GRAMMATICO**

The Foundations

Baby, now that I've found you

I can't let you go

I built my world around you

BABY, NOW THAT I'VE FOUND YOU	
1968	**JOHN MACLEOD, TONY MCCAULAY**

Why do you build me up

Buttercup baby, just to let me down

BUILD ME UP, BUTTERCUP	
1969	**TONY MCCAULEY, MICHAEL D'ABO**

lyrics are often embarrassed by print.

ROBERT HUNTER IN "BOX OF RAIN"

The Four Seasons

You better ask your mama

Sherry baby

Tell her everything is alright

SHERRY	
1962	**BOB GAUDIO**

I'm gonna walk like a man

Fast as I can

Walk like a man from you

WALK LIKE A MAN	
1963	BOB GAUDIO, BOB CREWE

Dawn, go away I'm no good for you...

Think, what the future would be with a poor boy like me

DAWN (GO AWAY)	
1964	SANDY LINZER, BOB GAUDIO

Silence is golden

But my eyes still see

SILENCE IS GOLDEN	
1964	BOB GAUDIO, BOB CREWE

And don't you worry 'bout me

I'll be strong, I'll try to carry on

OPUS 17 (DON'T WORRY 'BOUT ME)	
1966	DENNY RANDALL, SANDY LINZER

I keep working my way back to you

With a burning love inside

WORKING MY WAY BACK TO YOU	
1966	SANDY LINZER, DENNY RANDALL

Oh what a night, late December back in '63

What a very special time for me

DECEMBER 1963 (OH WHAT A NIGHT)	
1975	JUDY PARKER, BOB GAUDIO

The Four Tops

It's the same old song

But with a different meaning since you've been gone

IT'S THE SAME OLD SONG	
1965	BRIAN HOLLAND, LAMONT DOZIER, EDDIE HOLLAND

Standing in the shadows of love

I'm getting ready for the heartaches to come

STANDING IN THE SHADOWS OF LOVE	
1966	BRIAN HOLLAND, LAMONT DOZIER, EDDIE HOLLAND

Peter Frampton

Shadows grow so long before my eyes

And they're moving across the page

BABY I LOVE YOUR WAY	
1975	PETER FRAMPTON

I wonder if I'm dreaming, I feel so unashamed...

I watched you when you're sleeping

And I want to take your love

SHOW ME THE WAY	
1975	PETER FRAMPTON

Woke up this morning with a wine glass in my hand

Whose wine, what wine, where the hell did I dine?...

Come on, let's do it again

DO YOU FEEL LIKE WE DO	
1976	PETER FRAMPTON

Connie Francis

Where the boys are

Someone waits for me

WHERE THE BOYS ARE	
1961	HOWARD GREENFIELD

Fraternity of Man

Don't bogart that joint, my friend

Pass it over to me

DON'T BOGART THAT JOINT	
1967	ELLIOT INGBER, LARRY JAY WAGNER

Aretha Franklin

What you want baby I got it

What you need you know I got it

All I'm askin' for is a little respect

RESPECT	
1965, 1967	OTIS REDDING

Free

Hey what's your name baby

Maybe we can see things the same...

Let's move before they raise the parking rate

ALL RIGHT NOW	
1970	PAUL RODGERS, ANDY FRASER

Friends of Distinction

It sho' is mellow grazing in the grass

Grazing in the grass is a gas

Baby can you dig it?

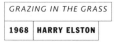

GRAZING IN THE GRASS	
1968	HARRY ELSTON

Bobby Fuller Four

I needed money 'cause I had none

I fought the law

And the law won

I FOUGHT THE LAW	
1966	BOBBY FULLER

Peter Gabriel

If looks could kill they probably will

In games without frontiers—war without tears

GAMES WITHOUT FRONTIERS	
1980	PETER GABRIEL

Marvin Gaye

Mother, mother, there's too many of you crying

Brother, brother, there's far too many of you dying

WHAT'S GOING ON	
1967, 1971	AL CLEVELAND, MARVIN GAYE, AND RENALDO BENSON

You could have told me yourself

That you loved someone else

Instead I heard it through the grapevine

I HEARD IT THROUGH THE GRAPEVINE	
1968	NORMAN WHITFIELD AND BARRETT STRONG

Too busy thinking about my baby

And I ain't got time for nothing else

TOO BUSY THINKING ABOUT MY BABY	
1969	NORMAN WHITFIELD, BARRETT STRONG, JANIE BRADFORD

If the spirit moves ya

Let me groove ya

Let's get it on

LET'S GET IT ON	
1973	MARVIN GAYE AND ED TOWNSEND

Gerry and the Pacemakers

So ferry, cross the Mersey

'Cause this land's the place I love

And here I'll stay

FERRY CROSS THE MERSEY	
1964	GERRY MARSDEN

125

⟶ 126

J. Geils Band

You got to give it to me

Why keep me cold when it's so warm inside

C'mon baby, your love is too good to hide

GIVE IT TO ME	
1973	PETER WOLF, SETH JUSTMAN

Jimmy Gilmer and the Fireballs

There's a crazy little house beyond the tracks

And ev'rybody calls it the Sugar Shack

SUGAR SHACK	
1963	KEITH MCCORMICK, FAYE VOSS

Golden Earring

I've been drivin' all night my hand's wet on the wheel

RADAR LOVE	
1974	BARRY HAY, GEORGE KOOYMANS

Leslie Gore

It's my party and I'll cry if I want to...

You would cry too if it happened to you

IT'S MY PARTY	
1963	HERB WEINER, WALLY GOLD, JOHN GLUCK, JR.

Grand Funk Railroad

Who wasn't there that you should look out for

Get back inside go on and shut the door

PARANOID	
1969	MARK FARNER

I'm your captain, I'm your captain

Though I'm feeling mighty sick

I'M YOUR CAPTAIN	
1970	MARK FARNER

Grand Funk's audience wasn't sensitive crowd. It was the guy dropped three downs, swigged a bottle Boone's Farm, and did a lot of out.

ROBERT DUNCAN IN "THE NOISE"

We're an American Band

We're comin' to your town

We'll help you party it down

WE'RE AN AMERICAN BAND	
1973	DON BREWER

Grass Roots

Sha la la la la la live for today

And don't worry about tomorrow

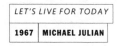

LET'S LIVE FOR TODAY	
1967	MICHAEL JULIAN

In my midnight confessions

When I tell all the world that I love you

MIDNIGHT CONFESSIONS	
1968	LOU JOSIE

She's got something that moves my soul and she knows

I'd love to love her...

Oh, temptation eyes, looking through my soul

TEMPTATION EYES	
1968	HARVEY PRICE, DAN WALSH

The Grateful Dead

It's just a box of rain...

Believe it if you need it

Or leave it if you dare

BOX OF RAIN	
1970	ROBERT HUNTER, PHIL LESH

We ponder the
thoughts of these

JERRY GARCIA, ON "DEADHEADS"

I set out running but I take my time

A friend of the devil is a friend of mine

If I get home before daylight

I just might get some sleep tonight

FRIEND OF THE DEVIL	
1970	**ROBERT HUNTER**

Sugar Magnolia, blossom's blooming

Heads are empty and I don't care

Saw my baby down by the river

Knew she had to come up soon for air...

She's got everything delightful

She's got everything I need

Takes the wheel when I'm seeing double

Pays my tickets when I speed...

She don't come and I don't follow

Waits back stage while I sing to you

SUGAR MAGNOLIA	
1970	**ROBERT HUNTER, BOB WEIR**

Your typical city involved in a typical daydream...

Sometimes the cards ain't worth a dime

If you don't lay'em down...

Sometimes the light's all shining on me

Other times I can barely see

Lately it occurs to me

What a long strange trip it's been

TRUCKIN'	
1970	**ROBERT HUNTER**

The Grateful Dead and others, at a press conference, complaining about police harrassment during a pot bust in 1967. The Dead said the law "was out of touch with reality."

L\R: Ron (Pig Pen) McKernon, Bill Kreutzmann, Phil Lesh, Rock Scully, Dan Rifkin, Bob Wier, Jerry Garcia, Michael Stepanion.

UPI/BETTMANN

Our audience doesn't come to see show-manship and theatrics. They realize what we are and that we're not performers and that we're a group that's earnestly trying to accomplish something and we don't quite know what it is.

JERRY GARCIA

people daily.

Keep on truck

Well the first days are the hardest days

Don't you worry any more

'Cause when life looks like Easy Street

There is danger at your door

UNCLE JOHN'S BAND	
1970	**ROBERT HUNTER**

Driving that train, high on cocaine

Casey Jones you'd better watch your speed

Trouble ahead, trouble behind

And you know that notion just crossed my mind

CASEY JONES	
1971	**ROBERT HUNTER**

Dobie Gray

Give me the beat boys and free my soul

I wanna get lost in your rock and roll

And drift away

DRIFT AWAY	
1973	**MENTOR WILLIAMS**

Norman Greenbaum

When I die and they lay me to rest

Gonna go to the place that's the best

SPIRIT IN THE SKY	
1970	**NORMAN GREENBAUM**

Guess Who

Seasons change and so did I

You need not wonder why...

There's no time left for you

NO TIME	
1970	**RANDY BACHMAN, BURT CUMMINGS**

in'.

CREATED BY ROBERT CRUMB

Do you know their names?

Can you play their games?

Without losing track and comin' down a bit too hard

SHARE THE LAND	
1970	BURT CUMMINGS

I don't know
like, how many of you can dig how many
people there are, man. Like, I was
rappin' to the fuzz. The New York
State Thruway is
closed, man.

ARLO GUTHRIE, AT WOODSTOCK

Arlo Guthrie

You can get anything you want at Alice's

Restaurant

ALICE'S RESTAURANT	
1966	ARLO GUTHRIE

Comin' into Los Angeles...

Don't touch my bags, if you please, Mr. Customs Man

COMING INTO LOS ANGELES	
1969	ARLO GUTHRIE

Good morning America how are you?

Don't you know me? I'm your native son

THE CITY OF NEW ORLEANS	
1972	ARLO GUTHRIE

Merle Haggard

We don't smoke marijuana in Muskogee

And we don't take our trips on L.S.D

And we don't burn our draft cards on Main Street

But we are living right and being free

And I'm proud to be an Okie from Muskogee

We don't make a party of loving

But we like holding hands and pitching woo...

Football's still the roughest thing on campus

And the kids here still respect the Dean

And I'm proud to be an Okie from Muskogee

OKIE FROM MUSKOGEE	
1969	**MERLE HAGGARD, ROY EDWARD BURRIS**

Bill Haley and the Comets

If the band slows down we'll yell for more

We're gonna rock around the clock tonight

ROCK AROUND THE CLOCK	
1953	**MAX FREEDMAN, JIMMY DE KNIGHT**

The first garage band? Probably not, but Bill Haley and the Comets are considered the first-ever rock 'n' roll band.

MICHAEL OCHS ARCHIVES

Get out from that kitchen

And rattle those pots and pans…

I said shake, rattle, and roll

SHAKE, RATTLE, AND ROLL	
1954	**CHARLES CALHOUN**

When I asked her what's the matter

This is what I heard her say

See you later alligator, after 'while, crocodile

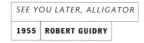

SEE YOU LATER, ALLIGATOR	
1955	**ROBERT GUIDRY**

Hall and Oates

Everybody's high on consolation

Everybody's tryin' to tell me what is right for me…

I need a drink and a quick decision

SHE'S GONE	
1974	**DARYL HALL, JOHN OATES**

You're a rich girl, and you've gone too far

'Cause you know it don't matter anyway

You can rely on the old man's money…

It's a bitch girl…

High and dry, out of the rain

It's so easy, to hurt others when you can't feel pain

RICH GIRL	
1977	**DARYL HALL, JOHN OATES**

Ain't no sign of weakness to give yourself away

Because the strong give up and move on

And the weak give up and stay

DO WHAT YOU WANT, BE WHAT YOU ARE	
1978	**DARYL HALL**

Albert Hammond

It never rains in California

But girl, don't they warn you

It pours, man it pours

IT NEVER RAINS IN CALIFORNIA	
1972, 1973	ALBERT HAMMOND, MIKE HAZELWOOD

The Happenings

There is danger in the summer moon above

Will I see you in September

Or lose you to a summer love?

SEE YOU IN SEPTEMBER	
1959, 1966	SID WAYNE

George Harrison

My friend came to me with sadness in his eyes

Told me that he wanted help before his country died

BANGLA-DESH	
1971	GEORGE HARRISON

You serve me and I'll serve you...

Bring your lawyer and I'll bring mine

SUE ME, SUE YOU BLUES	
1973	GEORGE HARRISON

Wilbert Harrison

I'm goin' to Kansas City

Kansas City here I come

They got some crazy little women there

And I'm gonna get me one

I'm gonna be standing on the corner

Twelfth Street and Vine

With my Kansas City baby

And a bottle of Kansas City wine

KANSAS CITY	
1959	JERRY LEIBER, MIKE STOLLER

Richie Havens

Freedom, freedom, freedom, freedom

Sometimes I feel, like a motherless child

A long, long, way, from my home, yeah

FREEDOM	
1968	**RICHIE HAVENS**

Isaac Hayes

That Shaft is a bad mother-

Shut your mouth!

Just talkin' 'bout Shaft

SHAFT	
1971	**ISAAC HAYES**

Heart

Seems like he knew me

He looked right through me

Come on home girl, he said with a smile

MAGIC MAN	
1976	**ANN WILSON, NANCY WILSON**

`You lying so low in the weeds

I bet you gonna ambush me

You'd have me down, down, down, down, on my knees

BARRACUDA	
1977	**ANN WILSON, NANCY WILSON, ROGER FISHER MICHAEL DEROSIER**

would fight like cats and dogs—over
or a note, or a phrase. It never came to
but it could get rough. MIKE STOLLER, ON WRITING SONGS WITH JERRY LEIBER

What the winner don't know

The gambler understands

STRAIGHT ON	
1978	**ANN WILSON, NANCY WILSON**

135

⟶ 136

Bobby Hebb

Sunny, yesterday my life was filled with rain

Sunny you smiled at me and really eased the pain

SUNNY

1965 | BOBBY HEBB

Jimi Hendrix

But first, are you experienced?

Ah, have you ever been experienced?

Well, I have

I know, I know you'll probably scream'n cry

That your little world won't let you go

But who in your measly little world

Are you trying to prove that

You're made out of gold and can't be sold...

Ah! but are you experienced?

Have you ever been experienced?

Not necessarily stoned, but beautiful

ARE YOU EXPERIENCED

1967 | JIMI HENDRIX

You don't care for me

I don'-a care about that

Gotta new fool, ha!

I like it like that

I have only one burning desire

Let me stand next to your fire

FIRE

1967 | JIMI HENDRIX

Hey Joe, where ya goin' with that gun in your hand?

I'm goin' out and shoot my old lady

HEY JOE

1967 | WILLIAM ROBERTS

"Scuse me while I kiss the sky":

Jimi Hendrix in concert.

MICHAEL OCHS ARCHIVES

Music sweet music I wish I could caress

Manic depression's a frustrating mess

MANIC DEPRESSION	
1967	JIMI HENDRIX

Purple haze was in my brain

Lately things don't seem the same

Actin' funny, but I don't know why

'Scuse me while I kiss the sky

Purple haze all around

Don't know if I'm coming up or down

Am I happy or in misery?

Whatever it is, that girl put a spell on me...

Is it tomorrow or just the end of time?

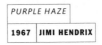

PURPLE HAZE	
1967	**JIMI HENDRIX**

A broom is drearily sweeping

Up the broken pieces of yesterday's life

Somewhere a Queen is weeping

Somewhere a King has no wife

And the wind it cries Mary...

Will the wind ever remember

The names it has blown in the past

And with this crutch, its old age, and its wisdom

It whispers, "No, this will be the last"—And the wind cries Mary

THE WIND CRIES MARY	
1967	**JIMI HENDRIX**

Anger he smiles, tow'ring in shiny metallic purple armor

Queen Jealousy, envy waits behind him

Her fiery green gown sneers at the grassy ground...

"Once happy turquoise armies lay opposite ready

But wonder why the fight is on

But they're all bold as love...

Just ask the Axis, he knows everything

You

BOLD AS LOVE	
1968	**JIMI HENDRIX**

There was a young girl whose heart was a frown

Because she was crippled for life and couldn't speak a sound

And she wished and prayed she would stop living

So she decided to die

She drew her wheel chair to the side of the shore

And to her legs she smiled "You won't hurt me no more"

But then a sight she'd never seen made her jump and say

"Look, a golden winged ship is passing my way"

And it really didn't have to stop

It just kept going

And so castles made of sand

Fall in the sea, eventually

CASTLES MADE OF SAND	
1968	**JIMI HENDRIX**

I'm not the only soul who's accused of hit and run

Tire tracks all across your back

Aha, I can see you had your fun...

You're just like crosstown traffic

(So hard to get through to you)

CROSSTOWN TRAFFIC	
1968	**JIMI HENDRIX**

can leave if you want to. I'm just jammin'.

JIMI HENDRIX AT WOODSTOCK

White collared conservative flashing down the street

Pointing their plastic finger at me

They're hoping my kind will drop and die

But I'm gonna wave my freak flag high, high

I'm the one who has to die when it's time for me to die

So let me live my life the way I want to…

If the sun refuse to shine

I don't mind, I don't mind

If the mountains fell in the sea

Let it be, it ain't me…

Got my own life to live through

And I ain't gonna copy you

IF SIX WAS NINE	
1968	JIMI HENDRIX

Well she's walking through the clouds

With a circus mind that's running wild…

When I'm sad she comes to me

With a thousand smiles she gives to me free

LITTLE WING	
1968	JIMI HENDRIX

It's very far away

It takes about a half a day to get there

If we travel by—dragonfly

SPANISH CASTLE MAGIC	
1968	JIMI HENDRIX

If I seem

And if I don't meet you no more in this world

Then I'll meet you in the next one

So don't be late

'Cause I'm a voodoo child

VOODOO CHILD	
1968	JIMI HENDRIX

Evil men make me kill you

Evil men make you kill me

Evil men make me kill you

Even tho' we're only fam'lies apart

Angel came down from heaven yesterday

She stayed with me just long enough to rescue me...

Then she spread her wings high over me

She said she's gonna come back tomorrow

And I said fly on my sweet angel

Fly on through the sky

Fly on my sweet angel

Tomorrow I'm gonna be by your side

A little boy inside a dream just the other day

His mind fell out of his face and the wind blew it away

A hand came down from heaven and pinned a badge on his chest

And said get out there man, and do your best

They called him Astro Man

And he's flyin' higher than that old faggot Superman ever could...

free it's because I'm always running.
JIMI HENDRIX

Well, I'm up here in this womb

I'm looking all around

Well I'm looking out my belly button window

And I see a whole lot of frowns

And I'm wond'rin' if they don't want me around...

Cause you know if they just don't want me this time around

141

Yea, I'll be glad to go back to spirit land.

So if there's any questions

Make up your mind…

Give or take

You only got 200 days

BELLY BUTTON WINDOW

1971 | JIMI HENDRIX

You all pass me that bottle

And I'll sing you a real song…

Now a lady with a pearl handled necktie

Tied to the driver's fence

Breathes in my face bourbon and coke possessed words

"Haven't I seen you somewhere in hell

Or was it just an accident?"

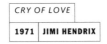

CRY OF LOVE

1971 | JIMI HENDRIX

Here comes Dolly Dagger

Her love's so heavy she's gonna make you stagger

Dolly Dagger, she drinks her blood from a jagged edge…

She gotta bullwhip just as long as your life

DOLLY DAGGER

1971 | JIMI HENDRIX

Drifting on a sea of forgotten teardrops

On a lifeboat sailing for your love

DRIFTING

1971 | JIMI HENDRIX

You got my pride hanging out of my bed

You're messing with my life, so I brought my lead

Even messing with my children

And you scream at my wife

Get off of my back

If you want to get out of here alive

Freedom, that's what I want now

Freedom, that's what I need now

Freedom to live

Freedom so I can give

FREEDOM

1971 | **JIMI HENDRIX**

Hello my friend, so happy to see you again...

Have you heard baby, what the wind's blowing down

Have you heard baby, a lot of people's coming right on down

Communication is coming on strong

Don't give a damn baby, if your hair is short or long

I said get out of your grave

Ev'rybody is dancing in the street

Do what you know and don't be slow

You gotta practice what you preach.

Forget about the past baby

Things ain't what they used to be

Keep on straight ahead

STRAIGHT AHEAD

1971 | **JIMI HENDRIX**

Don Henley

Out on the road today

I saw a Dead-head sticker on a Cadillac

A little voice inside my head said don't look back

THE BOYS OF SUMMER

1984 | **DON HENLEY**

Herman's Hermits

I'm Henry the Eighth, I am

'Enery the Eight, I am I am

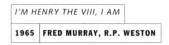

I'M HENRY THE VIII, I AM	
1965	FRED MURRAY, R.P. WESTON

Don't let on, don't say she broke my heart

I'd go down on my knees but it's no good to pine

MRS. BROWN, YOU'VE GOT A LOVELY DAUGHTER	
1965	TREVOR PEACOCK

There's a kind of hush all over the world tonight...

You can hear the sounds of lovers in love

THERE'S A KIND OF HUSH	
1966	LES REED, GEOFF STEPHENS

I'm leaning on the lampost at the corner of the street

In case a certain little lady comes by

LEANING ON THE LAMP POST	
1937, 1966	NOEL GAY

The Hollies

You can see the ladies in their gowns

When you look through any window

LOOK THROUGH ANY WINDOW	
1965	GRAHAM GOULDMAN, CHARLES SILVERMAN

Bus stop wet day she's there I say

Please share my umbrella

Bus comes bus goes she stays love grows

Under my umbrella

BUS STOP	
1966	GRAHAM GOULDMAN

Stop stop stop all the dancing

Give me time to breathe

STOP STOP STOP	
1966	**ALLAN CLARKE, TONY HICKS, GRAHAM NASH**

Where is your magic disappearing

Hey Carrie-Anne what's your game now

Can anybody play?

CARRIE-ANNE	
1967	**ALLAN CLARKE, GRAHAM NASH, TONY HICKS**

The road is long

With a many a winding turn

That leads us to who knows where

But I'm strong, strong enough to carry him

He ain't heavy, he's my brother...

His welfare is my concern

No burden is he to bear

We'll get there

HE AIN'T HEAVY, HE'S MY BROTHER	
1970	**BOB RUSSELL**

A pair of forty-fives made me open my eyes

My temperature started to rise

She was a long cool woman in a black dress

LONG COOL WOMAN (IN A BLACK DRESS)	
1972	**ROGER COOK, HAROLD CLARKE, ROGER GREENAWAY**

Buddy Holly and the Crickets

All my life I've been a-waitin'

Tonight there'll be no hesitatin'

OH BOY	
1957	**SONNY WEST, BILL TILGHMAN, NORMAN PETTY**

Oh Boy! Buddy Holly.

Peggy Sue, Peggy Sue

Oh how my heart yearns for you

PEGGY SUE	
1957	BUDDY HOLLY, JERRY ALLISON, NORMAN PETTY

You say you' gonna leave me...

'Cause that'll be the day, when I die

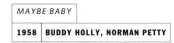

THAT'LL BE THE DAY	
1957	JERRY ALLISON, BUDDY HOLLY, NORMAN PETTY

Maybe baby, I'll have you

Maybe baby, you'll be true

MAYBE BABY	
1958	BUDDY HOLLY, NORMAN PETTY

Johnny Horton

Well we fired our guns but the British kept-a comin'

There wasn't as many as there was a while ago

We fired once more and they began a-runnin'

Down the Mississippi to the Gulf of Mexico...

We fired our cannon till the barrel melted down

So we grabbed an alligator and we fought another round

We filled his head with cannonballs and powdered his behind

And when we touched the powder off the gator lost his mind

BATTLE OF NEW ORLEANS	
1957	JIMMY DRIFTWOOD

Brian Hyland

Two three four, tell the people what she wore

"It was an itsy bitsy teenie weenie yellow polkadot bikini"

ITSY BITSY TEENIE WEENIE YELLOW POLKADOT BIKINI	
1960	PAUL J. VANCE, LEE POCKRISS

147

⟶ 148

'Tho we gotta say goodbye for the summer...

I'll send you all my love

Everyday in a letter, sealed with a kiss

SEALED WITH A KISS	
1962	**PETER UDEL**

Janis Ian

One of these days I'm gonna stop my listening

Gonna raise my head up high

SOCIETY'S CHILD (BABY I'VE BEEN THINKING)	
1966	**JANIS IAN**

And those of us with ravaged faces

Lacking in the social graces...

It isn't all it seems, at seventeen...

AT SEVENTEEN	
1974, 1975	**JANIS IAN**

Ides of March

I'm the friendly stranger in the black sedan

Oh won't you hop inside my car

VEHICLE	
1969	**JAMES M. PETERIK**

Iron Butterfly

In-A-Gadda-Da-Vida baby

Don't you know that I love you

IN-A-GADDA-DA-VIDA	
1965	**DOUG INGLE**

It's a Beautiful Day

But the white bird just sits in her cage

Growing old

White bird must fly or she will die

WHITE BIRD	
1969	**DAVID LA FLAMME, LINDA LA FLAMME**

Tommy James and the Shondells

My baby does the Hanky Panky

HANKY PANKY	
1966	JEFF BARRY, ELLIE GREENWICH

"Children behave," that's what they say

When we're together

And watch how you play

I THINK WE'RE ALONE NOW	
1967	RITCHIE CORDELL, BO GENTRY

Look over yonder, what do you see?

The sun is arising, most definitely

A new day is coming

CRYSTAL BLUE PERSUASION	
1969	TOMMY JAMES, MIKE VALE, ED GRAY

The James Gang

Seems to me, you don't want to talk about it...

You just turn your pretty head and walk away

WALK AWAY	
1971	JOE WALSH

Jan and Dean

Goin' to Surf City cause it's two to one

Two girls for every boy

SURF CITY	
1963	JAN BERRY, BRIAN WILSON

It's the little old lady from Pasadena

Go granny go, granny go, granny go

THE LITTLE OLD LADY (FROM PASADENA)	
1964	ROGER CHRISTIAN, DON ALTFELD

Jay and the Americans

Only in America, land of opportunity

Would a classy girl like you

Fall for a poor boy like me

ONLY IN AMERICA	
1963	JERRY LEIBER, CYNTHIA WEIL, MIKE STOLLER, BARRY MANN

Jay and the Techniques

Ready or not here I come

Gee that used to be such fun

APPLES, PEACHES, PUMPKIN PIE	
1967	MAURICE IRBY

Jefferson Airplane

When the truth is found to be lies

And all of the joy inside you dies...

Don't you want somebody to love?

SOMEBODY TO LOVE	
1967	DARBY SLICK

And one pill makes you small

And the ones that mother gives you

Don't do anything at all

WHITE RABBIT	
1967	GRACE SLICK

Look what's happening out in the streets...

One generation got old, one generation got soul

VOLUNTEERS	
1969	MARTY BALIN, PAUL KANTER

If you can remember any
you weren't really

Stoned consciousness darted, flowed, went where it wanted to go, freed of rectilinear purpose and instruction. Routine talk seemed laughable; juxtapositions made perfect sense. Meanwhile, virtually nothing was really weird, because anything might prove significant, or hilarious, or both.

JOHN HALL IN "THE SIXTIES"

AP/WIDE WORLD PHOTOS

thing about the Sixties, there.

PAUL KANTNER, JEFFERSON AIRPLANE

Jethro Tull

Sitting on a park bench

Eyeing little girls with bad intent...

Sun streaking cold

An old man wandering lonely

Taking time the only way he knows...

Aqualung my friend

Don't you start away uneasy

You poor old sod

You see it's only me...

And you snatch your rattling last breaths

With deep-sea diver sounds

And the flowers bloom like

Madness in the spring

AQUALUNG
1971 JENNIE ANDERSON

Who would steal the candy

From a laughing baby's mouth

If he could take it from the money man...

Laughing in the playground

Gets no kicks from little boys

Would rather make it with a letching grey

Or maybe her attention

Is drawn by Aqualung

Who watches through the railings as they play

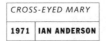

CROSS-EYED MARY
1971 IAN ANDERSON

If Jesus saves, well He'd better save Himself

From the gory glory seekers who use His name in death

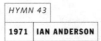

HYMN 43
1971 IAN ANDERSON

So lean upon Him gently

And don't call on Him to save you

From your social graces

And the sins you wish to waive

MY GOD

1971 | IAN ANDERSON

So I asked this God a question and by way of firm reply

He said, I'm not the kind you have to wind up on Sundays

So to my old headmaster (and to anyone that cares)

Before I'm through I'd like to say my prayers

I don't believe you; you got the whole damn thing all wrong

He's not the kind you have to wind up on Sundays

Well you can excommunicate me on my way to Sunday school

And have all the bishops harmonize these lines

How do you dare to tell me that I'm my father's son

When that was just an accident of birth

I'd rather look around me, compose a better song

'Cos that's the honest measure of my worth

WIND UP

1971 | IAN ANDERSON

Really don't mind if you sit this one out

My word's but a whisper, your deafness a shout

I may make you feel but I can't make you think

Your sperm's in the gutter, your love's in the sink

So you ride yourselves over the fields

And you make all your animal deals

And your wise men don't know how it feels

To be thick as a brick

THICK AS A BRICK

1972 | IAN ANDERSON

⟶ 154

The river is full of crocodile nasties

And he who made kittens put snakes in the grass

BUNGLE IN THE JUNGLE	
1974	IAN ANDERSON

Now he's too old to rock 'n' roll

But he's too young to die

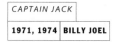

TOO OLD TO ROCK 'N' ROLL	
1974	IAN ANDERSON

Billy Joel

But Captain Jack will get you high tonight...

Captain Jack will get you by tonight

Just a little push and you'll be smilin'

CAPTAIN JACK	
1971, 1974	BILLY JOEL

He says, "Son can you play me a memory?

I'm not really sure how it goes

But it's sad and it's sweet and I knew it complete

When I wore a younger man's clothes."

Sing us a song, you're the piano man

Sing us a song tonight

Well we're all in the mood for a melody

And you've got us feelin' alright...

Yes they're sharing a drink they call loneliness

But it's better than drinking alone...

It's a pretty good crowd for a Saturday

And the manager gives me a smile

'Cause he knows that it's me they've

Been comin' to see to forget about life for awhile

And the piano sounds like a carnival

And the microphone smells like a beer

And they sit at the bar and put bread in my jar

And say, "Man, what are you doin' here?"

PIANO MAN	
1973, 1974	**BILLY JOEL**

From a town known as Oyster Bay, Long Island

Rode a boy with a six-pack in his hand

THE BALLAD OF BILLY THE KID	
1974	**BILLY JOEL**

I write the tunes first, then the lyrics, which are dictated by the mood of the music.

BILLY JOEL ON SONGWRITING

But that's alright my love...

Wherever we're together that's my home

YOU'RE MY HOME	
1974	**BILLY JOEL**

Everybody's talkin' 'bout the new sound

Funny, but it's still rock and roll to me

IT'S STILL ROCK AND ROLL TO ME	
1980	**BILLY JOEL**

You may be right

I may be crazy

But it just may be a lunatic you're looking for

YOU MAY BE RIGHT	
1980	**BILLY JOEL**

Well we're living here in Allentown

And they're closing all the factories down

Out in Bethlehem they're killing time

Filling out forms standing in line...

But they've taken all the coal from the ground

And the union people crawled away

Well I'm living here in Allentown

And it's hard to keep a good man down

But I won't be getting up today

And it's getting very hard to stay

ALLENTOWN

1981 | BILLY JOEL

We should all face up to what happened in Vietnam and show more com-
passion to the people who served
there. Whether it was right or
wrong, they laid their asses on the
line for us. And I think they got
the royal shaft for it.

BILLY JOEL

We passed the hash pipe

And played our Doors tape

And it was dark, so dark at night

And we held on to each other

Like brother to brother

Remember Charlie, remember Baker

They left their childhood on every acre

And who was wrong? And who was right?

It didn't matter in the thick of the fight...

Yes we would all go down together

GOODNIGHT SAIGON

1981 | BILLY JOEL

Elton John, in concert in Los Angeles.

Elton John

Holy Moses let us live in peace

Let us strive to make all hatred cease

There's a man over there

What's his color I don't care

He's my brother, let us live in peace

BORDER SONG	
1969	**ELTON JOHN, BERNIE TAUPIN**

⟶ 158

It seems to me a crime that we should age

These fragile times should never slip us by

A time you never can or shall erase

As friends together watch their childhood fly

FRIENDS

1970	ELTON JOHN, BERNIE TAUPIN

Take my word I'm a madman, don't you know

Once a fool had a good part in the play

If it's so would I still be here today

It's quite peculiar in a funny sort of way

The thing is very funny everything I say

Get a load of him he's so insane

Better get your coat, dear

It looks like rain

We'll come again next Thursday afternoon

The in-laws hope they'll see you very soon

MADMAN ACROSS THE WATER

1970	ELTON JOHN, BERNIE TAUPIN

Levon wears his war wound like a crown

He calls his child Jesus

'Cause he likes the name...

He was born a pauper to a pawn

On a Christmas day when the New York Times

Said God Is Dead and the war's begun

LEVON

1971	ELTON JOHN, BERNIE TAUPIN

Jesus freaks, out in the streets

Handing tickets out for God

Turning back, she just laughs

The boulevard is not that bad

TINY DANCER

1971	ELTON JOHN, BERNIE TAUPIN

I remember when rock was young

Me and Susie had so much fun

Holdin' hands and skimmin' stones

Had an old gold Chevy and a place of my own

CROCODILE ROCK	
1972	**ELTON JOHN, BERNIE TAUPIN**

Until I saw your city lights, honey I was blind

They said, "Get back honky cat

Better get back to the woods…"

Get back, honky cat

Livin' in the city ain't where it's at

It's like tryin' to find gold in a silver mine

It's like tryin' to drink whisky from a bottle of wine

HONKY CAT	
1972	**ELTON JOHN, BERNIE TAUPIN**

Spanish Harlem are not just pretty words to say

I thought I knew

But now I know that rose trees never grow

In New York City

MONA LISAS AND MAD HATTERS	
1972	**ELTON JOHN, BERNIE TAUPIN**

I'm not the man they think I am at home

I'm a rocket man

Rocket man, burning out his fuse up here alone…

And all this science I don't understand

It's just my job five days a week

ROCKET MAN (I THINK IT'S GOING TO BE A LONG LONG TIME)	
1972	**ELTON JOHN, BERNIE TAUPIN**

Oh Bennie she's really keen
She's got electric boots, a mohair suit
You know I read it in a magazine

BENNIE AND THE JETS	
1973	ELTON JOHN, BERNIE TAUPIN

Well it seems to me you lived your life
Like a candle in the wind
Never knowing who to cling to when the rain set in
And I would have liked to know you
But I was just a kid;
Your candle burned out long before your legend ever did

CANDLE IN THE WIND	
1973	ELTON JOHN AND BERNIE TAUPIN

It'll take you a couple of vodka and tonic's
To set you on your feet again
Maybe you'll get a replacement
There's plenty like me to be found
Mongrels, who ain't got a penny
Singing for tid-bits like you
So Goodbye Yellow Brick Road
Where the dogs of society howl
You can't plant me in your penthouse
I'm going back to my plough...
Oh, I've fin'lly decided my future lies
Beyond the Yellow Brick Road

GOODBYE YELLOW BRICK ROAD	
1973	ELTON JOHN, BERNIE TAUPIN

My old man's drunker than a barrel full of monkeys
And my old lady she don't care...
A couple of sounds that I really like

Are the sound of a switchblade and a motorbike

I'm a juvenile product of the working class

Whose best friend floats in the bottom of a glass

So don't give us none of your aggravation

We've had it with your discipline

Saturday night's alright for fightin'

SATURDAY NIGHT'S ALRIGHT (FOR FIGHTING)	
1973	ELTON JOHN, BERNIE TAUPIN

I can't light no more of your darkness

All my pictures seem to fade to black and white

I'm growing tired and time stands still before me

Frozen here on the ladder of my life...

But losin' ev'rything is like the sun goin' down on me

DON'T LET THE SUN GO DOWN ON ME	
1974	ELTON JOHN, BERNIE TAUPIN

You almost had your hooks in me, didn't you dear?

You nearly had me roped and tied, alter-bound, hypnotized;

Sweet freedom whispered in my ear, "You're a butterfly

And butterflies are free to fly, fly away, high away, bye bye"...

I never realized the passing hours of evening showers

A slip noose hanging in my darkest dreams

I'm strangled by your hunted social scene

Just a pawn out played by a dominating queen;...

And I would have walked head-on into the deep end of the river

Clinging to your stocks and bonds paying your H.P. demands forever

They're coming in the morning with a truck to take me home

SOMEONE SAVED MY LIFE TONIGHT	
1974	ELTON JOHN, BERNIE TAUPIN

I entertain by picking brains

Sell my soul by dropping names

I'm a bitch I'm a bitch, oh the bitch is back

Stone cold sober as a matter of fact

I'm a bitch I'm a bitch if I'm better than you

It's the way that I move, the fact that I do

THE BITCH IS BACK	
1975	ELTON JOHN, BERNIE TAUPIN

Lived here, he must have been a gardener that cared a lot

Who weeded out the tears and grew a good crop

And we are so amazed

We're crippled and we're dazed

A gardener like that one no one can replace

I've been knocking, but no one answers…

I've been calling, "Hey hey Johnny

Can't you come out to play?"

And through their tears

Some say he found his best in younger years

But he'd have said that roots grow stronger

If only he were here

EMPTY GARDEN (HEY, HEY JOHNNY)	
1982	ELTON JOHN, BERNIE TAUPIN

Jimmy Jones

Here is the main thing I want to say

I'm busy twenty four hours a day…

I'm your handy man

HANDY MAN	
1959	OTIS BLACKWELL, JIMMY JONES

But she had timin', timin'

Timin' is a thing it's true

Good timin' brought me to you

GOOD TIMIN'	
1960	CLINT BALLARD, JR., FRED TOBIAS

Joe Jones

You talk too much, you worry me to death

You talk too much, you even worry my pet

YOU TALK TOO MUCH	
1960	JOE JONES, REGGIE HALL

Janis Joplin

Down on me, down on me

Looks like everybody in this whole round world

Is down on me

DOWN ON ME	
1967	JANIS JOPLIN

Lord, won't you buy me a Mercedes-Benz

My friends all drive Porsches

I must make amends

MERCEDES-BENZ	
1970	JANIS JOPLIN

Janis Joplin, giving everything she has.

AP/WIDE WORLD PHOTOS

I'm sorry, babe. I just ain't got no more.

JANIS JOPLIN AT THE FILLMORE EAST, AFTER THE CROWD REFUSED TO LEAVE AFTER THREE ENCORES

Freedom's just another word for nothin' left to lose

And nothin' ain't worth nothin' if it ain't free...

ME AND BOBBY MCGEE	
1971	KRIS KRISTOFFERSON, FRED FOSTER

Journey

The wheel in the sky keeps on turning

I don't know where I'll be tomorrow

The wheel in the sky keeps me yearning

WHEEL IN THE SKY	
1978	NEAL SCHON, ROBERT FLEISCHMAN, DIANE VELORY

Kansas

Once I rose above the noise and confusion

Just to get a glimpse beyond the illusion

CARRY ON WAYWARD SON	
1976	KERRY LIVGREN

All we are is dust in the wind

Same old song

Just a drop of water in the endless sea

DUST IN THE WIND	
1977	KERRY LIVGREN

Ernie K-Doe

If she leaves us alone we would have a happy home

Sent from down below, mother-in-law

MOTHER-IN-LAW	
1961	ALLEN TOUSSAINT

Chris Kenner

C'mon let me show you where it's at

The name of the place: I like it like that

I LIKE IT LIKE THAT	
1961	CHRIS KENNER, ALLEN TOUSSAINT

Carole King

You make me feel like

A natural woman

(YOU MAKE ME FEEL LIKE) A NATURAL WOMAN	
1967	CAROLE KING

And it's too late, baby, it's too late...

Something inside has died and I can't hide

And I just can't fake it

IT'S TOO LATE	
1971	CAROLE KING

You can't talk to a man with a shotgun in his hand...

SMACKWATER JACK
1971 | CAROLE KING

So far away

Doesn't anybody stay in one place anymore?

It would be so fine to see your face at my door...

SO FAR AWAY
1971 | CAROLE KING

My life has been a tapestry of rich and royal hue

An everlasting vision of the everlasting view...

TAPESTRY
1971 | CAROLE KING

You just call out my name

And you know wherever I am

I'll come running...

YOU'VE GOT A FRIEND
1971 | CAROLE KING

The Kingsmen

Louie Louie, oh baby

Away got to go now

LOUIE, LOUIE
1963 | RICHARD BERRY

In the Top 40 half the songs are secret messages to the teen world to drop out, turn on, and groove with the chemicals and lightshows at discotheques.

ART LINKLETTER

165 ⟶ 166

The Kinks

Girl I want to be with you

All of the time

All day and all of the night

ALL DAY AND ALL OF THE NIGHT
1964 RAY DAVIES

Girl, you really got me going

You got me so I don't know what I'm doing

YOU REALLY GOT ME
1964 RAY DAVIES

Do what you like

But please don't keep me waiting

'Cause I'm so tired, tired of waiting for you

TIRED OF WAITING
1965 RAY DAVIES

He's a well respected man about town

Doing the best things so conservatively

WELL RESPECTED MAN
1965 RAY DAVIES

Well, I'm not dumb but I can't understand

Why she walked like a woman but talked like a man

LOLA
1970 RAY DAVIES

And when he feels the world closing in

He turns his stereo way up high...

Livin' in a rock and roll fantasy

A ROCK 'N' ROLL FANTASY
1978 RAY DAVIES

Kiss

You keep shoutin':

I wanna rock and roll all night

And party every day

ROCK AND ROLL ALL NITE	
1975, 1977	PAUL STANLEY, GENE SIMMONS

Beth I hear you callin'

But I can't come home right now...

Me and the boys are playin'

BETH	
1976	PETER CRISCUOLA, STANLEY PENRIDGE, BOB EZRIN

The Knack

Good girls don't

Good girls don't, but I do

GOOD GIRLS DON'T	
1979	DOUGLAS FIEGER

Such a dirty mind

I always get it up

For the younger kind

MY SHARONA	
1979	DON FIEGER, BESTON AVERRE

The Knickerbockers

Lies, lies, you're tellin' me that you'll be true

Lies, that's all I ever get from you

LIES	
1965	BUDDY RANDALL, BEAU CHARLES

Gladys Knight and the Pips

I'd rather live in his world

Than live without him in mine

MIDNIGHT TRAIN TO GEORGIA	
1973	JIM WEATHERLY

Kris Kristofferson

Don't say a word about tomorrow or forever...

And make believe you love me one more time

For the good times

FOR THE GOOD TIMES	
1968	KRIS KRISTOFFERSON

Bob Kuban and the In-Men

Look out for the cheater

He's gonna build you up

Just to let you down

THE CHEATER	
1965	JOHN KRENSKI, MIKE KRENSKI

Led Zeppelin

Good times bad times, you know I've had my share

When my woman left home with a brown-eyed man

Well, I still don't seem to care

GOOD TIMES BAD TIMES	
1969	JIMMY PAGE, JOHN PAUL JONES, JOHN BONHAM

Hey fellas have you heard the news

You know that Annie's back in town

It won't take long, just watch an' see

The fellas lay their money down

Her style is new but the face is the same

As it was so long ago

But from her eyes is a different smile

Like that of one who knows

HEARTBREAKER	
1969	**JIMMY PAGE, ROBERT PLANT, JOHN PAUL JONES, JOHN BONHAM**

Squeeze my lemon, till the juice runs down my leg

The way you squeeze my lemon

I swear I'm gonna fall right out of bed

THE LEMON SONG	
1969	**JIMMY PAGE, ROBERT PLANT, JOHN PAUL JONES, JOHN BONHAM, CHESTER BURNETT**

With a purple umbrella and a fifty cent hat

Livin', lovin', she's just a woman...

Alimony, alimony payin' your bills...

When your conscience hits you, knock it back with pills

Livin', lovin', she's just a woman

LIVING LOVING MAID (SHE'S JUST A WOMAN)	
1969	**JIMMY PAGE, ROBERT PLANT**

Ah, sometimes I grow so tired

But I know one thing I got to do

Ramble on—and now's the time to

Sing my song, I'm goin' round the world

I got to find my girl, on my way

RAMBLE ON	
1969	**JIMMY PAGE, ROBERT PLANT**

And so today, my world it smiles

Your hand in mine we walk the miles

THANK YOU	
1969	**JIMMY PAGE, ROBERT PLANT**

And if you say to me tomorrow

Oh what fun it all would be

Then what's to stop us, pretty baby

But what is and what should never be

I'm not

WHAT IS AND WHAT SHOULD NEVER BE	
1969	JIMMY PAGE, ROBERT PLANT

Way, way down inside

I'm gonna give you my love

I'm gonna give you every inch of my love...

Shake for me, girl

I wanna be your backdoor man

WHOLE LOTTA LOVE	
1969	JIMMY PAGE, ROBERT PLANT, JOHN PAUL JONES, JOHN BONHAM

I gotta woman who wants to ball all day

I gotta woman she won't be true

I gotta woman stays drunk all the time...

My little lover does a midnight shift

HEY HEY WHAT CAN I SAY	
1970	JIMMY PAGE, ROBERT PLANT, JOHN PAUL JONES, JOHN BONHAM

We come from the land of the ice and snow

From the midnight sun where the hot springs blow

IMMIGRANT SONG	
1970	JIMMY PAGE, ROBERT PLANT

Hey hey mama, said the way you move

Gonna make you sweat, gonna make you groove

Oh, oh child, way you shake that thing

Gonna make you burn, gonna make you sting...

I don't know but I been told

A big-legged woman ain't got no soul

BLACK DOG	
1972	JIMMY PAGE, JOHN PAUL JONES, JOHN BONHAM

Led Zeppelin. I'm just this 'character who keeps saying, 'I'm not Led Zeppelin'.

ROBERT PLANT

It's been a long time since I rock and rolled

It's been a long time since I did the stroll

Ooh, let me get it back, let me get it back, let me get it back...

Baby, where I come from

ROCK AND ROLL	
1972	JIMMY PAGE, ROBERT PLANT, JOHN PAUL JONES, JOHN BONHAM

There's a lady who's sure all that glitters is gold

And she's buying a stairway to heaven

And when she gets there she knows if the stores are closed

With a word she can get what she came for

STAIRWAY TO HEAVEN	
1972	ROBERT PLANT, JIMMY PAGE

Left Banke

Just walk away Renee

You won't see me follow you back home

The empty sidewalks on my block

Are not the same, you're not to blame

WALK AWAY, RENEE	
1966	MIKE LOOKOFSKY, TONY SANSONE, BOB CALILLI

The Lemon Pipers

Any song you want I'll gladly play

Money feeds my music machine

Now listen while I play my green tambourine

GREEN TAMBOURINE	
1967	SHELLEY PINZ, PAUL LEKA

John Lennon

Instant karma's gonna get you...

How in the world you gonna see

Laughin' at fools like me

Who in the world d'you think you are?

A superstar; Well alright you are...

Why in the world are we here?

Surely not to live in pain and fear

Why on earth are you there

When you're ev'rywhere

Come and get your share

Well we all shine on

INSTANT KARMA	
1970	**JOHN LENNON**

God is a concept by which we measure our pain

GOD	
1971	**JOHN LENNON**

So this is Christmas

And what have you done

Another year over, and a new one just begun...

And so this is Christmas

For weak and for strong

For rich and the poor ones

The world is so wrong

And so happy Christmas

For black and for white

For yellow and red ones

Let's stop all the fight

A very merry Christmas

Let's hope it's a good one

Without any fear

HAPPY XMAS (WAR IS OVER)	
1971	**YOKO ONO, JOHN LENNON**

If there were any

Imagine there's no countries

It isn't hard to do

Nothing to kill or die for

And no religion too...

You may say I'm a dreamer

But I'm not the only one

IMAGINE	
1971	**JOHN LENNON**

Power to the people

Power to the people, right on

POWER TO THE PEOPLE	
1971	**JOHN LENNON**

John Lennon was shot to death December 8, 1980. Most rock fans can relate to the pain and shock of this mourner as he sits in front of Lennon's Dakota apartment building listening to Beatle tapes.

AP/WIDE WORLD PHOTOS

We make her paint her face and dance

If she won't be a slave, we say that she don't love us

If she's real, we say she's tryin' to be a man

While putting her down we pretend that she's above us

Woman is the nigger of the world

WOMAN IS THE NIGGER OF THE WORLD	
1972	**JOHN LENNON, YOKO ONO**

illusions left at all for the children of the 60's, they too died Monday night— when the music died.

TIME, ON THE DEATH OF JOHN LENNON

We all been playing those mind games forever

Some kinda Druid dudes lifting the veil

Doing the mind guerilla

Some call it magic, the search for the grail...

(I want you to make love, not war

I know you've heard it before)

MIND GAMES	
1973	**JOHN LENNON**

173

⟶ 174

Nobody loves you when you're down and out

Nobody sees you when you're on Cloud Nine

NOBODY LOVES YOU (WHEN YOU'RE DOWN AND OUT)	
1973	JOHN LENNON

If it wasn't for John Lennon, a lot of us would be someplace much different tonight. It's a hard world that asks you to live a lot of things that are unlivable. And it's hard to come out here and play tonight.

BRUCE SPRINGSTEEN, IN CONCERT, AFTER THE DEATH OF JOHN LENNON

So long ago, was it in a dream?

Was it just a dream?...

Two spirits dancing so strange

Ah! bowakawa pusse, pusse

#9 DREAM	
1974	JOHN LENNON

Whatever gets you thru the night it's alright, it's alright

Don't need a sword to cut thru flowers, oh no, oh no,...

Don't need a watch to waste your time, oh no, oh no...

Don't need a gun to blow your mind, oh no, oh no

WHATEVER GETS YOU THRU THE NIGHT	
1974	JOHN LENNON

And you think you're so clever and classless and free

But you're still fucking peasants as far as I can see

WORKING CLASS HERO	
1979	JOHN LENNON

Life is what happens to you

While you're busy

Making other plans

BEAUTIFUL BOY (DARLING BOY)	
1980	JOHN LENNON

to replace someone like John.

PAUL MCCARTNEY

The queen is in the counting home

Counting out the money

The king is in the kitchen

Making bread and honey

However far we travel, wherever we may roam

The center of the circle, will always be our home

CLEANUP TIME	
1980	**JOHN LENNON**

Even after all these years

I miss you when you're not here...

After all is really said and done

The two of us are really one

The goddess really smiled upon our love dear Yoko

DEAR YOKO	
1980	**JOHN LENNON**

everybody telling me to do it? I already did it! JOHN LENNON

Our life together is so precious together

We have grown, we have grown...

We'll be together on our own again

Like we used to be in the early days...

It'll be just like starting over—starting over

(JUST LIKE) STARTING OVER	
1980	**JOHN LENNON**

Don't you miss the big time boy

You're no longer on the ball?

I'm just sitting here watching the wheels

Go round and round...

No longer riding on the merry-go-round

I just had to let it go

WATCHING THE WHEELS	
1980	**JOHN LENNON**

Woman I know you understand
The little child inside the man...
Woman please let me explain
I never meant to cause you sorrow or pain

WOMAN

1980 | JOHN LENNON

Like the Kennedys and King...except this time there was a difference. This time someone crawled out of a dark place, lifted a gun, and killed an artist. This was something new. This time, someone murdered a song.

NEW YORK MAGAZINE, ON THE DEATH OF JOHN LENNON

Gary Lewis and the Playboys

Who wants to buy this diamond ring?

She took it off her finger, now

It doesn't mean a thing

THIS DIAMOND RING	
1964	AL KOOPER, IRWIN LEVINE, BOB BRASS

Everybody loves a clown, so why don't you?

Everybody laughs at the things that I say and do

They all laugh when they see me comin'

But you don't laugh, you just go home runnin'

I guess I'm a clown that I don't want to be

Why can't you see the other side of me?

It's not easy to be, a clown, you see

When you're in love like me

EVERYBODY LOVES A CLOWN	
1965	GARY LEWIS, THOMAS LESSLIE, LEON RUSSELL

Jerry Lee Lewis

You shake my nerves and you rattle my brain

Too much love drives a man insane

GREAT BALLS OF FIRE	
1957	JACK HAMMER, OTIS BLACKWELL

Shake it baby shake it

Come on over

A whole lotta shakin' goin' on

WHOLE LOTTA SHAKIN' GOIN' ON	
1957	DAVE WILLIAMS AND SUNNY DAVID [ROY HALL]

"Whole, Lotta
Shakin' Goin On"
was my second record, and it was banned for
eight months. No one would have any
part of it. Then we got it on the
Steve Allen Show, and it
broke nationwide.

JERRY LEE LEWIS

Gordon Lightfoot

If you could read my mind, love

What a tale my thoughts could tell

Just like an old-time movie

'bout a ghost from a wishing well...

Just like a paperback novel

The kind the drugstore sells...

I'd walk away, like a movie star

Who gets burned in a three-way script

Enter number two: A movie queen

To play the scene of bringing all the good things out of me

IF YOU COULD READ MY MIND	
1969	**GORDON LIGHTFOOT**

Turnin' back the pages to the times I love best

I wonder if she'll ever do the same

Now the thing that I call livin' is just

Bein' satisfied with knowing I got no one left to blame

Carefree Highway, let me slip away on you

CAREFREE HIGHWAY	
1973, 1974	**GORDON LIGHTFOOT**

Sometimes, I think its a shame

When I get feelin' better when I'm feelin' no pain...

Sometimes I think it's a sin

When I feel like I'm winnin' when I'm losin again

SUNDOWN	
1973, 1974	**GORDON LIGHTFOOT**

Great Balls of Fire: Before he was ostracized by the public and the music industry for marrying his 13-year-old cousin, Jerry Lee Lewis was one of the hottest early rock stars.

MICHAEL OCHS ARCHIVES

The wind in the wires made a tattletale sound

And the wave broke over the railing

And every man knew as the captain did too

'Twas the witch of November comes stealing

At seven P.M. a main hatchway caved in

179

→ 180

He said, "Fellas, it's been good t' know ya!"...

"Superior" they said "never gives up her dead

When the gales of November come early!"

THE WRECK OF THE EDMUND FITZGERALD	
1976	GORDON LIGHTFOOT

Mark Lindsay

She must belong to San Francisco

She must have lost her way...

She says she believes in Robin Hood and brotherhood

And colors of green and gray

And all you can do is laugh at her

Doesn't anybody know how to pray?

Arizona, take off your rainbow shades

Arizona, have another look at the world my my

ARIZONA	
1969	KENNY YOUNG

Little Feat

I've been from Tucson to Tucumcari

From Tehachapi to Tonopah

Driven every kind of rig that's ever been made

Driven the back roads so I wouldn't get weighed

And if you give me weed, whites, and wine

And show me a sign I'll be willin'

WILLIN'	
1971	LOWELL GEORGE, MARTIN KIBBEE

People on LSD don't say where can I get more, a 7-11 store.
KEN KESEY, COMPARING LSD TO CRACK

I've seen the bright lights of Memphis

And the Commodore Hotel

And underneath a streetlamp I met a southern belle

She took me to the river where she cast her spell

And in that southern moonlight she sang this song so well

If you'll be my Dixie chicken I'll be your Tennessee lamb

And we can walk together down in Dixieland

DIXIE CHICKEN	
1973	**LOWELL GEORGE**

Little Richard

A-wop boppa lu bop a lop bomp bomp

I got a girl named Daisy

She almost drives me crazy

TUTTI FRUTTI	
1955	**RICHARD PENNIMAN, D. LABOSTRIE, JOE LUBIN**

I'm the real king of rock 'n' roll. I was singing rock before anybody knew what rock was back when swing music was the big thing. People like Elvis Presley, were the builders of rock 'n' roll— but I was the architect. ● **LITTLE RICHARD**

Gonna tell Aunt Mary 'bout Uncle John

He says he has the blues but he has a lot of fun

they don't rob   Oh baby

LONG TALL SALLY	
1956	**ENOTRIS JOHNSON, RICHARD PENNIMAN, ROBERT BLACKWELL**

181

⟶ 182

Good Golly Miss Molly, sure like to ball

Oh when you're rockin' and a-rollin'

Can you hear your mama call

GOOD GOLLY MISS MOLLY	
1958	JOHN MARASCALCO AND BUMPS BLACKWELL

I never actually knew a long tall Sally or an Uncle John. LITTLE RICHARD

It's about time: The self-proclaimed "architect of rock," Little Richard, clowns for photographers as he is inducted into L.A.'s Rock Walk for his lasting and continuous contributions to rock'n'roll.

AP/WIDE WORLD PHOTOS

Nils Lofgren

Well I ain't really that good looking I know...

It's my slippery fingers—that's all

SLIPPERY FINGERS	
1972	NILS LOFGREN

Dave Loggins

Ramblin' boy why don't you settle down

Boston ain't your kind of town

There ain't no gold and there ain't nobody like me

PLEASE COME TO BOSTON	
1974	DAVE LOGGINS

Loggins and Messina

What a shot you would be if

You could shoot at me with those angry eyes

ANGRY EYES	
1972, 1973	JIM MESSINA AND KENNY LOGGINS

Your mama don't dance and

Your daddy don't rock and roll

YOUR MAMA DON'T DANCE	
1972	KENNY LOGGINS AND JIM MESSINA

Lovin' Spoonful

Do you believe in magic

In a young girl's heart

How the music can free her

Whenever it starts...

I'll tell you 'bout the magic and it'll free your soul

But it's like tryin' to tell a stranger 'bout a rock and roll

DO YOU BELIEVE IN MAGIC?	
1965	JOHN SEBASTIAN

183

⟶ 184

She's one of those girls

Who seems to come in the spring

One look in her eyes and you forget everything

You were ready to say

And I saw her today

YOUNGER GIRL

1965 | **JOHN SEBASTIAN**

What a day for a daydream

What a day for a daydreamin' boy

Now I'm lost in a sweet dream

Dreamin' about my bundle of joy

And even if time ain't really on my side

It's one of those days for taking a walk outside

DAYDREAM

1966, 1967 | **JOHN SEBASTIAN**

Did you ever have to make up your mind?

And pick up on one and leave the other behind

It's not often easy and not often kind

DID YOU EVER HAVE TO MAKE UP YOUR MIND?

1966 | **JOHN SEBASTIAN**

All around people lookin' half dead

Walkin' down the sidewalk, hotter than a match head

Cool cat, lookin' for his kitty

Gonna look in every corner of the city

SUMMER IN THE CITY

1966 | **JOHN SEBASTIAN, STEVE BOONE, MARK SEBASTIAN**

Lulu

A friend that taught me right from wrong

And weak from strong, that's a lot to learn

But what can I give you in return

TO SIR WITH LOVE	
1967	DON BLACK

Lynyrd Skynyrd

Cause I'm as free as a bird now

And this bird you cannot change

FREE BIRD	
1973	ALLEN COLLINS AND RONNIE VAN ZANT

Gimme me three steps

Gimme me three steps mister

Gimme me three steps toward the door

GIMME THREE STEPS	
1973	ALLEN COLLINS, RONNIE VAN ZANT

Well I hope Mr. Young will remember

That southern man don't need him around anyhow

SWEET HOME ALABAMA	
1974	EDWARD KING, GARRY ROSSINGTON, RONNIE VAN ZANT

Lynyrd Skynrd was named after Leonard Skinner, a gym teacher at Robert E. Lee High School in Jacksonville who hassled the group about their long hair.

You got a barrel that's blue and cold

Ain't good for nothing

Except to put a man six feet in a hole

SATURDAY NIGHT SPECIAL	
1975	EDWARD KING, RONNIE VAN ZANT

185   ⟶ 186

The Live Aid famine relief concert at Wembley Stadium, in London: L\R: Pete Townshend, David Bowie, Linda and Paul McCartney, and the organizer, Bob Geldof, among many others. The U.S. site of the Live Aid concert was Philadelphia.

A/P WIDE WORLD PHOTOS

Whiskey bottles and brand new cars...

There's too much coke and too much smoke...

The smell of death surrounds you

THAT SMELL	
1977	ALLEN COLLINS AND RON VAN ZANT

Paul McCartney [and Wings]

Give Ireland back to the Irish

Don't make them have to take it away...

GIVE IRELAND BACK TO THE IRISH	
1972	PAUL MCCARTNEY

If I ever get out of here

Thought of giving it all away...

All I need is a pint a day

BAND ON THE RUN	
1974	PAUL AND LINDA MCCARTNEY

Maybe I'm amazed at the way you love me all the time

Maybe I'm afraid of the way I love you

MAYBE I'M AMAZED	
1976	PAUL MCCARTNEY

Save the planet, man. I need it for later.

PAUL MCCARTNEY, SPEAKING FOR HIS INFANT SON

The McCoys

Sloopy, I don't care what your daddy do...

Hang on Sloopy, Sloopy hang on

HANG ON SLOOPY	
1964	BERT RUSSELL, WES FARELL

Apocalypse Later: GI's of the Firebase Catherine organize a rock session, surrounded by symbols of the war—wooden bunkers, helicopters, and sandbags. They are dug in on a hill south of the DMZ in the northernmost portion of South Vietnam.

There has been no song remotely like this one in the decade-long history of rock music. strident and bitter, its references blatantly topical. JOHN HALL, ON "THE EVE OF DESTRUCTION," IN "THE SIXTIES"

Barry McGuire

You're old enough to kill, but not for votin'...

And tell me, over and over and over again my friend

You don't believe we're on the eve of destruction

EVE OF DESTRUCTION

1965 | PHIL F. SLOAN

189 ⟶ 190

Scott McKenzie

If you're going to San Francisco

Be sure to wear some flowers in your hair...

All across the nation, such a strong vibration

SAN FRANCISCO (BE SURE TO WEAR SOME FLOWERS IN YOUR HAIR)	
1967	SCOTT MCKENZIE

Don McLean

Something touched me deep inside

The day the music died

AMERICAN PIE	
1971	DON MCLEAN

You took your life as lovers often do

But I could have told you Vincent

This world was never meant for one as beautiful as you

VINCENT	
1971	DON MCLEAN

Madonna

I have a tale to tell

Sometimes it gets so hard

To hide it well

LIVE TO TELL	
1986	MADONNA AND PAT LEONARD

I'm crazy for you

Touch me once and you'll know it's true

CRAZY FOR YOU	
1985	JOHN BETTIS AND JON LIND

Mamas and Papas

All the leaves are brown, and the sky is grey...

California dreamin' on such a winter's day

CALIFORNIA DREAMIN'	
1965	JOHN PHILLIPS

in, turn on, drop out.
TIMOTHY LEARY

Monday, Monday can't trust that day

Monday, Monday sometimes it just turns out that way

MONDAY MONDAY	
1966	JOHN PHILLIPS

Words of love

So so soft and tender

Won't win a girl's heart anymore

WORDS OF LOVE	
1966	JOHN PHILLIPS

McGuinn and McGuire are-a just-a gettin' higher

In L.A. you know where that's at

And no one's gettin' fat except mama Cass

CREEQUE ALLEY	
1967	JOHN PHILLIPS, MICHELLE GILLIAM

Go where you wanna go

Do what you wanna do

GO WHERE YOU WANNA GO	
1967	JOHN PHILLIPS

191   ⟶ 192

Manfred Mann

There she was just a-walkin' down the street...

Singin' do wah diddy diddy dum diddy do

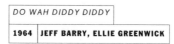

DO WAH DIDDY DIDDY	
1964	JEFF BARRY, ELLIE GREENWICK

Barry Mann

I'd like to thank the guy

Who wrote the song...

Who put the bomp in the bomp ba bomp ba bomp?

WHO PUT THE BOMP	
1961	BARRY MANN, GERRY GOFFIN

Bob Marley

Get up, stand up

Stand up for your rights...

Never give up the fight

GET UP, STAND UP	
1973	BOB MARLEY

You never leave the bus. Nobody ever leaves the bus. The bus may spit you out for a while, but nobody ever leaves the bus. KEN KESEY

I shot the sheriff

But I swear it was in self-defense

I SHOT THE SHERIFF	
1974	BOB MARLEY

We're leaving Babylon

We're going to our Father's land

MOVEMENT OF JAH PEOPLE	
1977	BOB MARLEY

Martha and the Vandellas

Could it be the devil in me

Or is this the way love's supposed to be

Like a heat wave

HEAT WAVE	
1963	**EDDIE HOLLAND, BRIAN HOLLAND, LAMONT DOZIER**

Are you ready for a brand new beat?

Summer's here and the time is right

For dancing in the street

DANCING IN THE STREET	
1966	**WILLIAM STEVENSON AND MARVIN GAYE**

Marvelettes

Well if the fish isn't on your line

Bait your hook and keep on trying...

Too many fish in the sea

TOO MANY FISH IN THE SEA	
1964	**EDDIE HOLLAND, NORMAN WHITFIELD**

Please Mister Postman look and see

Is there a letter in your bag for me?...

PLEASE MR. POSTMAN	
1961	**BRIAN HOLLAND, FREDDY GORMAN**

Dave Mason

Seems I've got to have a change of scene

Cause every night I have the strangest dreams

FEELIN' ALRIGHT	
1968	**DAVE MASON**

There ain't no good guy

There ain't no bad guy

There's only you and me and we just disagree

WE JUST DISAGREE	
1977	**JIM KRUEGER**

⟶ 194

My body aches for you to just be here

You are every woman in the world to me

EVERY WOMAN IN THE WORLD	
1980	**DOMINIC BUGATTI AND FRANK MUSTER**

Curtis Mayfield

Freddie's dead, that's what I said

Let the man with the plan say he'd send him home

But his hope was a rope

And he should have known

It's hard to understand there was love in this man...

Everybody's misused him, ripped him up and abused him

Another junkie plan, pushin' dope for the man

A terrible blow but that's how it goes...

We're all filled up with progress

But sometimes I must confess

We can deal with rockets and dreams

But reality, what does it mean

Ain't nothin' said, cause Freddie's dead...

Don't wanna be like Freddy now —cause Freddie's dead

If you try, you're gonna die...

No one's serious, and it makes me furious

Don't be misled

Just think of Fred

FREDDIE'S DEAD	
1972	**CURTIS MAYFIELD**

Superfly, you're gonna make your fortune by and by

But if you lose, don't ask no questions why

SUPERFLY	
1972	**CURTIS MAYFIELD**

MC 5

(Right now it's time to—

Kick out the jams motherfucker)

Well I feel pretty good

And I guess that I could get crazy now baby...

The girls can't stand it when they're doin' it right

They must understand, then they kick out the jams

Yes I'm startin' to sweat

And now my shirt's all wet

What I'm feeling

In the sound that abounds

And resounds and rebounds off the ceiling

KICK OUT THE JAMS	
1969	R. TYNER, M. DAVIS, D. TOMICH, F.D. SMITH, W. KAMBES

Meat Loaf

[Boy]: Though it's cold and lonely in the deep dark night

I can see paradise by the dashboard light...

[Girl]: Ain't no doubt about it

We were doubly blessed

Cause we were barely seventeen

And we were barely dressed...

[Boy]: We're gonna go all the way tonight...

[Girl]: Stop right there!

I gotta know right now!

Before we go any further, Do you love me?

Will you love me forever?

[Boy]: Let me sleep on it

Baby, baby, let me sleep on it

Let me sleep on it

And I'll give you the answer in the morning...

[Girl]: I gotta know right now!...

[Boy]: I couldn't take it any longer

Lord I was crazed

And when the feeling came upon me

Like a tidal wave

I started swearing to my god and on my mother's grave

That I would love you till the end of time

I swore that I'd love you till the end of time!

So now I'm praying for the end of time

To hurry up and arrive

Cause if I gotta spend another minute with you

I don't think that I can really survive

PARADISE BY THE DASHBOARD LIGHT	
1977	JIM STEINMAN

I want you

I need you

But—there ain't no way I'm ever gonna love you

Now don't be sad

'Cause two out of three ain't bad...

You'll never find your gold on a sandy beach

You'll never drill for oil on a city street

I know you're looking for a ruby in a mountain of rocks

But there ain't no Coupe de Ville hiding at the bottom

Of a Cracker Jack Box

TWO OUT OF THREE AIN'T BAD	
1977	JIM STEINMAN

John Cougar Mellencamp

He's got an interstate running through his front yard

You know he thinks he's got it so good

PINK HOUSES	
1983	JOHN MELLENCAMP

Lee Michaels

Been fourteen years since I saw her

I just saw her with my best friend

Do you know what I mean?

DO YOU KNOW WHAT I MEAN?	
1971	LEE MICHAELS

Buddy Miles

Well my mind is goin' through them changes

I think I'm goin' out of my mind

Everytime you see me goin' somewhere

I think I could go anytime

THEM CHANGES	
1967	BUDDY MILES

Steve Miller

I'm a joker, I'm a smoker, I'm a midnight toker

THE JOKER	
1973, 1976	STEVE MILLER

The Mindbenders

Wouldn't you agree, baby you and me

Got a groovy kind of love

GROOVY KIND OF LOVE	
1966	TONI WINE, CAROLE BAYER SAGER

The Miracles

Keep your freedom for as long as you can

My mama told me, "You better shop around"

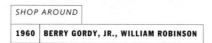

SHOP AROUND	
1960	BERRY GORDY, JR., WILLIAM ROBINSON

Joni Mitchell

I've looked at love from both sides now

From give and take, win and lose

And still somehow:

It's love's illusions that I recall

I really don't know love at all

BOTH SIDES NOW

1967 | **JONI MITCHELL**

They paved paradise

And put up a parking lot

With a pink hotel

A boutique, and a swinging hot spot

BIG YELLOW TAXI	
1969	JONI MITCHELL

I came upon a child of God; he was walking along the road

And I asked him "Where are you going?"

This he told me: "I'm going on down to Yasgur's Farm

Gonna join in a rock and roll band

I'm gonna camp out on the land and try 'n' get my soul free."

We are stardust we are golden

And we got to get ourselves back to the garden

By the time we got to Woodstock we were half a million strong

And everywhere was song and celebration

And I dreamed I saw the bombers riding shotgun in the sky

Turning into butterflies above our nation

WOODSTOCK	
1969	JONI MITCHELL

Maybe it's been too long a time

Since I was scrambling down in the street

And I've gotten used to that clean white linen

And that fancy French cologne

Carey get out your cane

I'll put on my finest silver

Boy you're a mean old daddy

But I like you

CAREY	
1971	JONI MITCHELL

The last time I saw Richard was Detroit in '68

And he told me

How romantics meet the same fate someday

Cynical and drunk

And boring someone in some cafe

"You laugh," you said, "You think you're immune

Go look at your eyes, a fallen moon

You like roses and kisses and pretty men

To tell you all those pretty lies"

All the dreamers pass this way someday

Hidin' behind bottles in dark cafes

THE LAST TIME I SAW RICHARD

1971 | **JONI MITCHELL**

Drivin' into town with a dark cloud above you

Dialin' the number who's bound to love you

Oh honey, you turn me on, I'm a radio

I'm a country station, I'm a little bit corny…

I know you don't like weak women

You get bored so quick

And you don't like strong women

'Cause they're hip to your tricks…

Cause who needs the static

It hurts the head

And you wind up crackin'

And the day goes dismal

If your head says forget it

But your heart's still smokin'

Call me at the station

The lines are open

YOU TURN ME ON I'M A RADIO

1972 | **JONI MITCHELL**

And the kids were wonderful. It was "Sir this," and "Sir that" and "thank you this" and "thank you that." Nobody can complain about the kids. This thing was too big—it was too big for the world. Nobody has ever seen a thing like this.

SIDNEY, A 76-YEAR-OLD ANTIQUE STORE OWNER, AT WOODSTOCK

I was a free man in Paris

I felt unfettered and alive

Nobody was callin' me up for favors

And no one's future to decide

You know I'd go back there tomorrow

But for the work I've taken on

Stokin' the star maker machin'ry

Behind the popular songs

FREE MAN IN PARIS

1973, 1974 | JONI MITCHELL

Good morning people! An area resident offers hot coffee to bedraggled music fans in Monticello, New York.

UPI/BETTMANN NEWSPHOTOS

Help me I think I'm falling, in love again

When I get that crazy feeling I know I'm in trouble again

He was sitting in the lounge of the Empire Hotel

He was drinking for diversion

He was thinking of himself

I was driving across the burning desert

When I spotted six jet planes

Leaving six white vapor trails across the bleak terrain

It was the hexagram of the heavens

It was the strings of my guitar

Amelia, it was just a false alarm...

The drone of flying engines

Is a song so wild and blue

It scrambles time and seasons if it gets thru to you

Then your life becomes a travelogue

Of picture-post-card-charms

Amelia, it was just a false alarm...

A ghost of aviation

She was swallowed by the sky

Or by the sea, like me she had a dream to fly

Like Icarus ascending

On beautiful foolish arms

Amelia, it was just a false alarm

Maybe I've never really loved

I guess that is the truth

I've spent my whole life in clouds at icy altitudes

And looking down on everything

I crashed into his arms

Amelia, it was just a false alarm

I pulled into the Cactus Tree Motel

To shower off the dust

And I slept on the strange pillows of my wanderlust

I dreamed of 747's

Over geometric farms

Dreams, Amelia, dreams and false alarms

AMELIA

1976 **JONI MITCHELL**

I've got a blue motel room

With a blue bedspread

I've got the blues inside and outside my head

Will you still love me

When I get back to town

BLUE MOTEL ROOM

1976 **JONI MITCHELL**

He's got another woman down the hall

He seems to want me anyway

Why'd you have to get so drunk

And lead me on that way

You just picked up a hitcher

A prisoner of the white lines on the freeway...

Of the fine white lines

Of the white lines on the free, free way

COYOTE

1976 **JONI MITCHELL**

I'm travelling in some vehicle

I'm sitting in some cafe

A defector from the petty wars

That shell shock love away

There's comfort in melancholy

When there's no need to explain

HEJIRA

1976 **JONI MITCHELL**

203

⟶ 204

I met a friend of spirit

He drank and womanized

And I sat before his sanity

I was holding back from crying

He saw my complications

And he mirrored me back simplified

And we laughed how our perfection

Would always be denied

REFUGE IN THE ROADS

1976 | JONI MITCHELL

A woman I knew just drowned herself

The well was deep and muddy

She was just shaking off futility

Or punishing somebody

My friends were calling up all day yesterday

All emotions and abstractions

It seems we all live so close to that line

And so far from satisfaction

Dora says, "Have children!"

Mama and Betsy say—"Find yourself a charity

Help the needy and the crippled

Or put some time into ecology"

Well there's a wide wide world of noble causes

And lovely landscapes to discover

But all I really want to do, right now

Is... find another lover!...

You sing for your friends and your family

I'll walk green pastures by and by

SONG FOR SHARON

1976 | JONI MITCHELL

Molly Hatchet

Don't try to turn my head away

Flirtin' with disaster every day

FLIRTIN' WITH DISASTER	
1979	DAVID LAWRENCE HLUBEK, BANNER HARVEY THOMAS, DANNY JOE BROWN

Eddie Money

I'm gonna take you on a trip so far from here

I've got two tickets in my pocket, baby

We're gonna disapear

Waiting so long

I've got two tickets to paradise

Won't you pack your bags, we'll leave tonight

TWO TICKETS TO PARADISE	
1977	EDDIE MONEY

The Monkees

Here we come walkin' down the street

We get the funniest looks from everyone we meet

MONKEES THEME	
1966	TOMMY BOYCE, BOBBY HART

There comes a time when you have to draw the line as a man. We're being passed off as something we aren't. We all play instruments, but we didn't on any of our records up to then. Furthermore, our company doesn't want us to. MICHAEL NESMITH

Finally in New York, the yelling for us got so bad during Jimi's set that he walked off stage. He was in the middle of a number. He threw his guitar down, flipped everyone the bird, said, "Fuck you," and walked off the stage. I was standing with Mickey Dolenz, and I turned to Mickey and I said, "Good for him... MICHAEL NESMITH, ABOUT JIMI HENDRIX, THE OPENING ACT DURING A MONKEES TOUR

Come with me leave yesterday behind

And take a giant step outside your mind

TAKE A GIANT STEP	
1966	CAROLE KING, GERRY GOFFIN

I thought love was only true in fairy tales

And for someone else, but not for me...

Then I saw her face

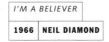

I'M A BELIEVER	
1966	NEIL DIAMOND

Cheer up sleepy Jean

Oh what can it mean

To a daydream believer and a homecoming queen

DAYDREAM BELIEVER	
1967	JOHN STEWART

Another pleasant valley Sunday...

Rows of houses that are all the same

And no one seems to care

PLEASANT VALLEY SUNDAY	
1967	CAROLE KING, GERRY GOFFIN

The Monotones

Oh I wonder, wonder, who, who who wrote the book of love?

BOOK OF LOVE	
1957	WARREN DAVIS, GEORGE MALONE, CHARLES PATRICK

The Moody Blues

I'm looking at myself, reflections of my mind

It's just the kind of day to leave myself behind

Look, no amps! The Monkees jamming, 1966.

AP/WIDE WORLD PHOTOS

TUESDAY AFTERNOON	
1968	JUSTIN HAYWARD

Tell us what you've seen

In far away forgotten lands

Where empires have turned back to sand

LOVELY TO SEE YOU
1969 | **JUSTIN HAYWARD**

If only you knew what's inside of me now

You wouldn't want to know me somehow

NEVER COMES THE DAY
1969 | **JUSTIN HAYWARD**

Wake up in the morning to yourself

And leave this crazy world behind you

DAWNING IS THE DAY
1970 | **JUSTIN HAYWARD**

My mind becomes confused

Between the dead and the sleeping

And the road I must choose

QUESTION
1970 | **JUSTIN HAYWARD**

Listen to the tide slowly turning

Wash all our heartaches away

THE STORY IN YOUR EYES
1971 | **JUSTIN HAYWARD**

I'm just a singer in a rock and roll band

How can we understand

Lies by the people for the people who

Are only destroying themselves

I'M JUST A SINGER (IN A ROCK AND ROLL BAND)
1973 | **JOHN LODGE**

Van Morrison

G-L-O-R-I-A, Gloria

I'm gonna shout all night

GLORIA

| 1965 | **VAN MORRISON** |

Well it's a marvelous night for a moondance...

A fantabulous night to make romance

MOONDANCE

| 1970 | **VAN MORRISON** |

Mott the Hoople

Television man is crazy

Says we're juvenile delinquent wrecks

Oh, man, I need TV when I got T. Rex...

And my brother's back at home

With his Beatles and his Stones

We never got it off on that revolution stuff

What a drag, too many snags

I've drunk a lot of wine and I'm feeling fine...

Is that concrete all around

Or is it in my head

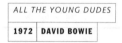

ALL THE YOUNG DUDES	
1972	**DAVID BOWIE**

Mungo Jerry

When the weather's fine

You got women, you got women on your mind

Have a drink, have a drive

Go out and see what you can find

IN THE SUMMERTIME	
1970	**RAY DORSET**

Music Explosion

Now when you're feeling low

And the fish won't bite

You need a little bit o' soul

To put you right

You gotta make like you wanna kneel and pray

And then a little bit o'soul will come your way

LITTLE BIT O' SOUL	
1967	**JOHN SHAKESPEARE, KENNETH LEWIS**

Violence
understand.

Napoleon XIV

They're coming to take me away ho ho

Hee-hee, ha-ha

To the funny farm where life is beautiful all the time

THEY'RE COMING TO TAKE ME AWAY, HA-HAAA!	
1966	**ROSEMARY DJIVRE**

Graham Nash

So your brother's bound and gagged

And they've chained him to a chair

Won't you please come to Chicago

CHICAGO	
1971	**GRAHAM NASH**

Military madness is killing the country

So much sadness

Is killing me

MILITARY MADNESS	
1971	**GRAHAM NASH**

seems to be the only thing we
The system will not yet yield without a fight, and it will react
only if the people with the power
begin to fear those
who have
nothing to lose.

WILLIAM KUNSTLER

Rick Nelson

Poor little fool oh yeah

I was a fool uh huh

POOR LITTLE FOOL	
1958	**SHARI SHEELEY**

Hello Mary Lou, goodbye heart

HELLO MARY LOU

1961 | GENE PITNEY

Pretty Polynesian baby over the sea
I remember the night
When we walked in the sand of Waikiki

TRAVELIN' MAN

1961 | JERRY FULLER

But it's alright now
I've learned my lesson well
You see you can't please everyone
So you got to please yourself...
If you gotta play at Garden parties
I wish you a lot a' luck
But if memories were all I sang
I'd rather drive a truck

GARDEN PARTY

1972 | RICK NELSON

Randy Newman

Scarecrows dressed in the latest styles
With frozen smiles to chase love away
Human kindness is overflowing
And I think it's going to rain today

I THINK IT'S GOING TO RAIN TODAY

1955 | RANDY NEWMAN

They all hate us anyhow
So let's drop the big one now
Let's drop the big one now

POLITICAL SCIENCE

1969 | RANDY NEWMAN

How we laugh up here in heaven

At the prayers you offer me

That's why I love mankind

GOD'S SONG (THAT'S WHY I LOVE MANKIND)	
1972	RANDY NEWMAN

In America you get food to eat

Won't have to run through the jungle and scuff up your feet...

In America every man is free

To take care of his home and his family

You'd be as happy as a monkey in a monkey tree

Sail away, sail away

We will cross the mighty ocean into Charleston Bay

SAIL AWAY	
1972	RANDY NEWMAN

Short people got no reason to live...

They got little baby legs

And they stand so low

You got to pick'em up

Just to say hello...

They got grubby little fingers

And dirty little minds

They're gonna get you every time

SHORT PEOPLE	
1977	RANDY NEWMAN

Americans dream of gypsies, I have found...

And African appendages that almost reach the ground

And little boys playing baseball in the rain

America, America, step out into the light

You're the best dream man has ever dreamed

And may all your Christmases be white

SIGMUND FREUD'S IMPERSONATION OF ALBERT EINSTEIN IN AMERICA	
1977	RANDY NEWMAN

213

> **"I've been accused of getting Nixon elected, the rise of conservatism, and crack terrorists holding Manhattan hostage. Now, all of this is true. But it's only a small part of my work."** ABBIE HOFFMAN

They say that money

Can't buy love in this world

But it'll get you a half-pound of cocaine

And a sixteen-year-old girl...

Now that may not be love

But it is all right

IT'S MONEY THAT I LOVE	
1979	**RANDY NEWMAN**

Harry Nilsson

I'm going where the sun keeps shining

Through the pouring rain

Going where the weather suits my clothes

EVERYBODY'S TALKING	
1967	**FRED NEIL**

Yippie leader Abbie Hoffman at a news conference at the Federal Building in Chicago. In the middle of the Democratic Convention, Hoffman offered to leave town for $100,000, according to an aide of Mayor Richard Daley.

AP/WIDE WORLD PHOTOS

By

Phil Ochs

Show me the prison, show me the jail...

And there but for fortune go you or I

THERE BUT FOR FORTUNE	
1963	**PHIL OCHS**

I'm sure it wouldn't interest anybody

Outside of a small circle of friends

A SMALL CIRCLE OF FRIENDS	
1967	**PHIL OCHS**

The O'Kaysions

I'm a girl watcher

Watching girls go by, my oh my

I'm a girl watcher, here comes one now

GIRL WATCHER	
1968	BUCK TRAIL [RONALD KILLETTE]

Yoko Ono

Save your sweet talk for when you score...

I want the truth and nothing more

I'M MOVING ON	
1980	YOKO ONO

Roy Orbison

Only the lonely know the way I feel tonight

Only the lonely know this feeling ain't right

ONLY THE LONELY	
1960	ROY ORBISON, JOE MELSON

the time I started recording, they would say to me, "Do you read music?" And I'd say, "Not enough to hurt my pickin'."

ROY ORBISON

Some rock 'n' roll reinforces friendship and community. Roy's ballads were always best when you were alone in the dark. (His songs) addressed the underside of pop romance. They were scary.

BRUCE SPRINGSTEEN, ON ROY ORBISON

In dreams... I talk to you

In dreams... you're mine, all of the time

IN DREAMS	
1963	ROY ORBISON

I don't believe you, you're not the truth

No one could look as good as you, mercy

OH, PRETTY WOMAN	
1964	**ROY ORBISON**

Robert Parker

Take off your shoes and pat your feet

We're doing a song that can't be beat

We're barefootin'

BAREFOOTIN'	
1965	**ROBERT PARKER**

Carl Perkins

Do anything you wanna do

But unh unh honey lay off of my shoes

BLUE SUEDE SHOES	
1955	**CARL PERKINS**

Peter, Paul and Mary

A dragon lives forever, but not so little boys

Painted wings and giant rings make way for other toys

PUFF (THE MAGIC DRAGON)	
1963	**PETER YARROW, LEONARD LIPTON**

But if I really say it

The radio won't play it

Unless I lay it between the lines

I DIG ROCK AND ROLL MUSIC	
1967	**PAUL STOKEY, JAMES MASON, DAVE DIXON**

All my bags are packed, I'm ready to go

I'm standin' here outside your door...

I'm leavin' on a jet plane

Don't know when I'll be back again

Oh babe I hate to go

LEAVING ON A JET PLANE	
1967	**JOHN DENVER**

Peter and Gordon

Lock me away

And don't allow the day, here inside

WORLD WITHOUT LOVE	
1964	**JOHN LENNON, PAUL MCCARTNEY**

Seventeen a beauty queen

She made a ride that caused a scene in the town

Her long blonde hair

Hanging down around her knees

All the cats who dig striptease

Praying for a little breeze...

Hey Lady Godiva

Her long blonde hair

Falling across her arms

Hiding all the lady's charms

LADY GODIVA	
1966	**MIKE LEANDER, CHARLES MILLS**

Tom Petty and the Heartbreakers

Baby even the losers get lucky sometimes

EVEN THE LOSERS	
1979	**TOM PETTY**

Everybody's got to fight to be free

You see you don't have to live like a refugee

REFUGEE	
1980	**TOM PETTY, MIKE CAMPBELL**

Bobby Pickett and the Crypt Kickers

He did the mash, (He did the Monster Mash)...

It was a graveyard smash

Wilson Pickett

I'm gonna wait till the midnight hour

When there's nobody else around

All you want to do is ride around Sally

Ride, Sally, ride

Pink Floyd

You lock the door

and throw away the key

There's someone in my head but it's not me...

Money so they say

Is the root of all evil today

MONEY	
1973	ROGER WATERS

The sun is the same in the relative way, but you're older

Shorter of breath and one day closer to death...

Hanging on in quiet desperation is the English way

With, without

And who'll deny it's what the fighting's all about

The establishment, especially in America, has absorb the revolution. Rock music is big business. The of the record companies are part of the power structure—they're friends of the police. Revolution—as a word, not an act—has become very fashionable.

MICHELANGELO ANTONIONI

We're just knocked out. We heard about the sell out. You gotta get an album out,

You owe it to the people. We're so happy we can hardly count.

And did we tell you the name of the game, boy, we call it riding

the gravy train

What did you dream? It's all right, we told you what to dream.

You dreamed of a big star, he played a mean guitar,

He always ate in the Steak Bar. He loved to drive his Jaguar.

WELCOME TO THE MACHINE

| 1975 | ROGER WATERS |

So you think you can tell Heaven from Hell, blue skies from pain.

Can you tell a green field from a cold steel rail? A smile from a veil?

Do you think you can tell?

And did they get you to trade your heroes for ghosts? Hot ashes for trees?

Hot air for a cool breeze? Cold comfort for change?

And did you exchange a walk on part in the war for a lead role in a cage?...

Running over the same old ground. What have we found? The same old fears.

Wish you were here

We don't need no education

We don't need no thought control...

Hey teacher, leave those kids alone

ANOTHER BRICK IN THE WALL (PART 2)	
1979	ROGER WATERS

Hey you! Out there on your own

Sitting naked by the phone

Would you touch me...

Open your heart, I'm coming home...

But it was only fantasy

The wall was too high, as you can see

No matter how he tried he could not break free...

Hey you! Out there on the road

Always doing what you're told

Can you help me?

Hey you!... Don't tell me there's no hope at all

Together we stand, divided we fall

THE WALL	
1979	ROGER WATERS

Nigel and

Gene Pitney

And so I cry a little bit, to be in love

Die a little bit, to be in love

IT HURTS TO BE IN LOVE	
1964	HOWARD GREENFIELD, HELEN MILLER

The Platters

Oh yes, I'm the great pretender...

My need is such, I pretend too much

THE GREAT PRETENDER	
1955	BUCK RAM

The Police

Roxanne, you don't have to wear that dress tonight

Walk the streets for money

I don't care if it's wrong or if it's right

ROXANNE	
1979	**STING**

Every breath you take, every move you make...

I'll be watching you

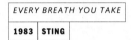

EVERY BREATH YOU TAKE	
1983	**STING**

David are like two great poets, like Keats and Shelley. They are like fire and ice. I see myself somewhere in the middle—like lukewarm water.

DEREK SMALLS IN THE FILM, THIS IS SPINAL TAP

Elvis Presley

Don't be cruel, to a heart that's true...

I really love you baby, cross my heart

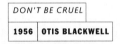

DON'T BE CRUEL	
1956	**OTIS BLACKWELL**

Well since my baby left me

Well I found a new place to dwell

Well it's down at the end of lonely street

At Heartbreak Hotel

HEARTBREAK HOTEL	
1956	**M.B. AXTON, TOMMY DURDEN, ELVIS PRESLEY**

If I could find a white boy who could sing like a (negro), I could make a million bucks.

SAM PHILLIPS, OWNER OF SUN RECORDS

221   ⟶ 222

Well you ain't never caught a rabbit
And you ain't no friend of mine

HOUND DOG	
1956	JERRY LEIBER, MIKE STOLLER

"If it had
bly be

Love me tender, love me sweet
Never let me go

LOVE ME TENDER	
1956	ELVIS PRESLEY, VERA MATSON

Well bless my soul what's a-wrong with me
I'm itchin' like a man on a fuzzy tree

ALL SHOOK UP	
1957	OTIS BLACKWELL, ELVIS PRESLEY

The King in his prime.

THE BETTMANN ARCHIVE

Warden threw a party in the county jail
The prison men were there and they began to wail...
Let's rock, everybody let's rock
Everybody in the whole cell block
Was dancin' to the jailhouse rock...
If you can't find a partner use a wooden chair
Let's rock, everybody let's rock
Everybody in the whole cell block
Was dancin' to the jailhouse rock

JAILHOUSE ROCK	
1957	JERRY LEIBER, MIKE STOLLER

Wise men say, only fools rush in

But I can't help falling in love with you

I CAN'T HELP FALLING IN LOVE	
1962	**GEORGE WEISS, HUGO PERETTI, LUIGI CREATORE**

I write I'm sorry

But my letter keeps coming back

RETURN TO SENDER	
1962	**OTIS BLACKWELL, WINFIELD SCOTT**

n't been for Elvis, I'd proba-
driving a snowplow in „
Minneapolis." PRINCE

The man
never had a
bad take.
One was
better than
the other.
He was like
an Olympic
champion.
He could
sing all
day.

JERRY LEIBER, ON ELVIS PRESLEY

Not bad, guys. Elvis Presley examines the latest offering of Mike Stoller and Jerry Leiber, "Jailhouse Rock," at MGM Studios in California, 1957. Leiber and Stoller, one of the most prolific songwriting teams of rock, continued churning out hit after hit not only for Elvis, but also for the Coasters, the Drifters, Ben E. King, and others.

LEIBER AND STOLLER ARCHIVES

And his mama cries

'Cause if there's one thing that she don't need

It's another hungry mouth to feed, in the ghetto

IN THE GHETTO (THE VICIOUS CIRCLE)	
1969	**MAC DAVIS**

⟶ 224

The Pretenders

Gonna use my style, gonna use my senses

Gonna use my fingers, gonna use my imagination

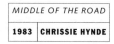

BRASS IN POCKET	
1979	CHRISSIE HYNDE, J.H. SCOTT

I'm not the kind I used to be

I've got a kid, I'm 33

MIDDLE OF THE ROAD	
1983	CHRISSIE HYNDE

Prince

When you were mine

How I used to let you wear all of my clothes...

I love you more than I did when you were mine

WHEN U WERE MINE	
1980	PRINCE

I was dreamin' when I wrote this

Forgive me if it goes astray...

Two thousand, zero, zero, party over out of time

So tonight I'm gonna party like it's nineteen ninety nine

1999	
1982	PRINCE

Prince in concert.

I guess I should have closed my eyes
When you drove me to the place
Where your horses run free
I felt a little ill when I saw all the
pictures
Of the jockeys that were there
before me

Believe it or not I started to worry
Wondering if I had enough class
But it was Saturday night
I guess that makes it alright.
Little red corvette
Baby you're much too fast

LITTLE RED CORVETTE

1983 | PRINCE

225

John Prine

There's a hole in daddy's arm

Where all the money goes

SAM STONE	
1971	JOHN PRINE

Out on the street I couldn't tell
the Vietnam veterans from the rock
and roll veterans. The Sixties had
made so many casualties, its war
and its music had run power off the
same circuit for so long they
didn't even have to fuse.

MICHAEL HERR IN "BREATHING OUT"

But much to my surprise

When I opened my eyes

I was a victim of the Great Compromise

THE GREAT COMPROMISE	
1972	JOHN PRINE

Procol Harum

Conquistador, there is no time

I must pay my respects...

You did not conquer, only die

CONQUISTADOR	
1967	KEITH REID

We skipped the light fandango

Turned cartwheels 'cross the floor

I was feeling kind of seasick

A WHITER SHADE OF PALE	
1967	KEITH REID

Gary Puckett and the Union Gap

There's nothing I can do

But spend all of my time out of my mind over you

OVER YOU	
1968	**JERRY FULLER**

A woman has a special look

When she's on the move...

Woman, have you got cheating on your mind?

WOMAN, WOMAN	
1968	**JAMES W. GLASER, JAMES PAYNE**

Young girl get out of my mind

My love for you is way out of line

You better run girl, you're much too young girl

YOUNG GIRL	
1968	**JERRY FULLER**

Pure Prairie League

Amie what you wanna do?

Fallin' in and out of love with you

Don't know what I'm gonna do

AMIE/FALLIN' IN AND OUT	
1975	**CRAIG FULLER**

Queen

I've paid my dues, time after time

I've done my sentence, but committed no crime...

WE ARE THE CHAMPIONS	
1977	**FREDDIE MERCURY**

She leaves me in a cold cold sweat

I gotta be cool, relaxed

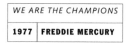

A CRAZY LITTLE THING CALLED LOVE	
1979	**FREDDIE MERCURY**

Out of the doorway the bullets rip

Repeating the sound of the beat

ANOTHER ONE BITES THE DUST	
1980	JOHN DEACON

R.E.O Speedwagon

So if you're tired of the same old story

Oh, turn some pages

I'll be here when you are ready

KEEP ON LOVING YOU	
1980	KEVIN CRONIN

Gerry Rafferty

He's got this dream about buying some land

He's gonna give up the booze and the one night stands

BAKER STREET	
1978	GERRY RAFFERTY

Otis Redding

Oh, she may be weary

Young girls they do get weary

Wearing that same old shaggy dress

One chord is Three

TRY A LITTLE TENDERNESS	
1966	6REG CONNELLY, HARRY WOODS, JIMMY CAMPBELL

Now I'm just gonna sit at the dock of the bay

Watchin' the tide roll away

SITTIN' ON THE DOCK OF THE BAY	
1968	STEVE CROPPER, OTIS REDDING

You always hear stories about celebrities saying it's bad to take fame and success too seriously—that it's dumb to believe all the hype. I never understood what they meant. But after I went through it, and did it wrong, I finally understood exactly what they were talking about.

KEVIN CRONIN, REO

Helen Reddy

I am woman hear me roar

In numbers too big to ignore

And I know too much to go back and pretend

I AM WOMAN	
1971	HELEN REDDY

Should I bring him down

Should I scream and shout

Should I speak of love, let my feelings out?

I DON'T KNOW HOW TO LOVE HIM	
1971	TIM RICE

Lou Reed

Plucked her eyebrows on the way

Shaved her legs and then he was a she, she said

"Hey babe, take a walk on the wild side..."

WALK ON THE WILD SIDE	
1972	LOU REED

fine. Two chords are pushing it. chords and you're into jazz.

LOU REED, ON ROCK 'N' ROLL

Paul Revere and the Raiders

Well you got this need to know what I'm all about

Well there's something that you dig you can't figure out

HUNGRY	
1965	BARRY MANN, CYNTHIA WEILL

⟶ 230

Don't it seem like kicks

Just keep gettin' harder to find

KICKS	
1966	BARRY MANN, CYNTHIA WEILL

Tim Rice

Ev'rytime I look at you I don't understand

Why you let the things you did get so out of hand

SUPERSTAR	
1969	TIM RICE

Mitch Ryder and the Detroit Wheels

She's a real humdinger and I like her like that

Devil with the Blue dress, blue dress, blue dress

DEVIL WITH A BLUE DRESS ON & GOOD GOLLY MISS MOLLY (MEDLEY)	
1966	FREDERICK LONG, WILLIAM STEVENSON

The Righteous Brothers

Time goes by so slowly

And time can do so much

Are you still mine?

UNCHAINED MELODY	
1955, 1965	HY ZARET

You never close your eyes anymore

When I kiss your lips

YOU'VE LOST THAT LOVIN' FEELING	
1964	BARRY MANN, CYNTHIA WEILL, PHIL SPECTOR

You're my soul and my heart's inspiration

Without you baby, what good am I

(YOU'RE MY) SOUL AND INSPIRATION	
1966	BARRY MANN, CYNTHIA WEILL

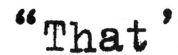

Johnny Rivers

And girl it's hard to find nice things

On the poor side of town

POOR SIDE OF TOWN	
1966	JOHNNY RIVERS, LOU ADLER

There's a man who leads a life of danger...

Secret agent man...

Giving you a number and taking away your name

SECRET AGENT MAN	
1966	PHIL SLOAN, STEVE BARRI

The Rivingtons

Papa-Oom-Mow-Mow

Corniest sound I ever heard

I can't understand a single word

PAPA-OOM-MOW-MOW	
1962	AL FRAZIER, CARL WHITE, TURNER WILSON, JOHN HARRIS

Smokey Robinson and the Miracles

And maybe you'll go away and never call

And a taste of honey's worse than none at all

I SECOND THAT EMOTION	
1967	WILLIAM ROBINSON, ALFRED CLEVELAND

Now if there's a smile upon my face

It's only there trying to fool the public

TEARS OF A CLOWN	
1967	HENRY COSBY, WILLIAM "SMOKEY" ROBINSON, STEVIE WONDER

s righteous, brother."

A DISC JOCKEY'S DESCRIPTION OF AN EARLY BILL MEDLEY AND BOBBY HATFIELD PERFORMANCE—THE GENESIS FOR THE NAME RIGHTEOUS BROTHERS.

The Rolling Stones

Hey hey, you you

Get off of my cloud

GET OFF MY CLOUD	
1965	MICK JAGGER, KEITH RICHARDS

I can't get no satisfaction

I can't get no girl reaction

(I CAN'T GET NO) SATISFACTION	
1965	MICK JAGGER, KEITH RICHARDS

She goes running for the shelter

Of a mother's little helper

MOTHER'S LITTLE HELPER	
1966, 1967	MICK JAGGER, KEITH RICHARDS

Well nothin' I do don't seem to work

It only seems to make matters worse…

Here it comes…

19TH NERVOUS BREAKDOWN	
1966	MICK JAGGER, KEITH RICHARDS

I'm not too good at pulling strings—12
6 is my

I see a red door and I want it painted black

No colors anymore I want them to turn back

PAINT IT BLACK	
1966	MICK JAGGER, KEITH RICHARDS

Don't you worry 'bout what's on your mind

I'm in no hurry I can take my time

LET'S SPEND THE NIGHT TOGETHER	
1967	MICK JAGGER, KEITH RICHARDS

I've got nasty habits, I take tea at three

LIVE WITH ME	
1967, 1969	MICK JAGGER, KEITH RICHARDS

Lose your dreams and you

Will lose your mind

Ain't life unkind?

RUBY TUESDAY	
1967	MICK JAGGER, KEITH RICHARDS

Please allow me to introduce myself

I'm a man of wealth and taste

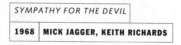

SYMPATHY FOR THE DEVIL	
1968	MICK JAGGER, KEITH RICHARDS

Oh a storm is threat'ning my very life today

If I don't get some shelter

I'm gonna fade away

GIMME SHELTER	
1969	MICK JAGGER, KEITH RICHARDS

You can't always get what you want

But if you try sometimes...

You get what you need

is my maximum, specialty.
KEITH RICHARDS

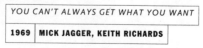

YOU CAN'T ALWAYS GET WHAT YOU WANT	
1969	MICK JAGGER, KEITH RICHARDS

Well, we all need someone we can lean on

And if you want it, well you can lean on me

LET IT BLEED	
1969	MICK JAGGER, KEITH RICHARDS

Please sister morphine turn my nightmare into a dream

SISTER MORPHINE	
1969, 1971	MICK JAGGER, KEITH RICHARDS

Please allow me to introduce myself: The Rolling Stones performing on the Ed Sullivan Show, 1966.

And you can send me dead flowers ev'ry morning

No I won't forget to put roses on your grave

DEAD FLOWERS	
1970, 1971	MICK JAGGER, KEITH RICHARDS

I have my freedom

But I don't have much time

WILD HORSES	
1970, 1971	MICK JAGGER, KEITH RICHARDS

thirty. Never trust anybody

ANON

Rarely had rock music invoked such to hell.

TIME MAGAZINE, IN A REVIEW OF THE ALBUM, "STICKY FINGERS"

Yeah when you call my name

I salivate like a Pavlov dog...

BITCH	
1971	MICK JAGGER, KEITH RICHARDS

Beating cold English blood runs hot

Lady of the house wond'rin' where it's gonna stop

BROWN SUGAR	
1971	MICK JAGGER, KEITH RICHARDS

With no loving in our souls

And no money in our coats

You can't say we're satisfied

ANGIE	
1973	MICK JAGGER, KEITH RICHARDS

I know it's only rock and roll

But I like it

IT'S ONLY ROCK AND ROLL	
1975	**MICK JAGGER, KEITH RICHARDS**

The Rover Boys

A time we'll treasure thru the years

We'll remember always graduation day

GRADUATION DAY	
1956	**NOEL SHERMAN**

over

an invitation

Roxy Music

Oh, mother of pearl, submarine lover in a shrinking world

MOTHER OF PEARL	
1974	**BRYAN FERRY**

I say go; she say yes;

Dim the lights

You can guess the rest

LOVE IS THE DRUG	
1975	**BRYAN FERRY, ANDY MACKAY**

Then I see you coming...

Much communication in a motion

Without conversation or a notion

AVALON	
1982	**BRYAN FERRY**

Bill Joe Royal

People put me down

But that's the part of town

I was born in

DOWN IN THE BOONDOCKS	
1965	**JOE SOUTH**

237

⟶ 238

Royal Guardsmen

Ten, twenty, thirty, forty, fifty or more

The bloody red baron was rollin' up the score

SNOOPY VS. THE RED BARON	
1966	PHIL GERNHARD, RICHARD L. HOLLER

Jimmy Ruffin

I walk in shadows searching for light

Cold and alone, no comfort in sight

WHAT BECOMES OF THE BROKEN-HEARTED?	
1966	JAMES DEAN, PAUL RISER, WILLIAM WEATHERSPOON

Todd Rundgren

I take for granted that you just don't care

Sometimes I can't help seeing all the way through

HELLO IT'S ME	
1969	TODD RUNDGREN

We gotta get you a woman

It's like nothing else to make you

Feel sure you're alive

WE GOTTA GET YOU A WOMAN	
1970	TODD RUNDGREN

Rush

And the men who hold high places

They must be the ones to start

Mold a new reality

Closer to the heart

The blacksmith and the artist

Practice in their art

They forge their creativity

Closer to the heart

CLOSER TO THE HEART	
1977	NEAL PEART, PETER TALBOT

Leon Russell

I'm up on the tightwire

One side's ice and one is fire

It's a circus game with you and me

TIGHTROPE	
1972	LEON RUSSELL

Safaris

Ooh ooh ooh ah aha ah... wipeout

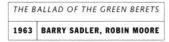

WIPEOUT	
1963	RON WILSON, JAMES FULLER, ROBERT BERRYHILL, PATRICK CONNOLLY

Barry Sadler

Back at home a young wife waits

Her Green Beret has met his fate

He has died for those oppressed

THE BALLAD OF THE GREEN BERETS	
1963	BARRY SADLER, ROBIN MOORE

Buffy Sainte-Marie

I'm not a queen, I'm a woman

Take my hand, we'll make a space

UNTIL IT'S TIME FOR YOU TO GO	
1965	BUFFY SAINTE-MARIE

Sam and Dave

I'm a soul man...

Grab the rope and I'll pull you in

Give you hope and be your only boyfriend

SOUL MAN	
1967	ISAAC HAYES, DAVID PORTER

You didn't have to love me like you did

But you did, but you did

And I thank you

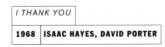

I THANK YOU	
1968	ISAAC HAYES, DAVID PORTER

Sam the Sham and the Pharaohs

Matty told Hatty about a thing she saw

Had two big horns and a wooly jaw

WOOLY BULLY	
1965	DOMINGO SAMUDIO

Hey there Little Red Riding Hood...

You're everything that a big bad wolf could want

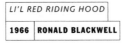

LI'L RED RIDING HOOD	
1966	RONALD BLACKWELL

Santana

When I come home, baby

My house is dark and my thoughts are cold

EVIL WAYS	
1970	CLARENCE HENRY

Leo Sayer

I am a man of the roads a hobo by name

I don't seek entertainment

Just poultry and game

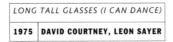

LONG TALL GLASSES (I CAN DANCE)	
1975	DAVID COURTNEY, LEON SAYER

Boz Scaggs

Georgia, your daddy was high

The night he dreamed of you

GEORGIA	
1976	BOZ SCAGGS

Dawn came in this morning

Like some old junkyard melody

HARBOR LIGHTS	
1976	**BOZ SCAGGS**

He'll be makin' like a feline

Headin' for the borderline

Goin' for broke

LIDO SHUFFLE	
1976	**BOZ SCAGGS, DAVID PAICH**

You ain't got to be so bad, got to be so cold

This dog eat dog livin' is surely gettin' old

LOWDOWN	
1976	**BOZ SCAGGS, DAVID PAICH**

Hope they never end this song

This could take us all night long

LOOK WHAT YOU DONE TO ME	
1980	**BOZ SCAGGS, DAVID FOSTER**

Seals and Croft

Summer breeze makes me feel fine

Blowin' thru the jasmine in my mind

SUMMER BREEZE	
1971	**JAMES SEALS**

The Searchers

I held my nose I closed my eyes

I took a drink

I didn't know if it was day or night

I started kissing everything in sight

But when I kissed a cop down on 34th and Vine

He broke my little bottle of love potion number nine

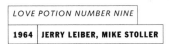

LOVE POTION NUMBER NINE	
1964	**JERRY LEIBER, MIKE STOLLER**

241

Neil Sedaka

They say that breakin' up is hard to do

Now I know, I know that it's true

BREAKING UP IS HARD TO DO	
1962	HOWARD GREENFIELD, NEIL SEDAKA

Pete Seeger

Where have all the soldiers gone? Long time ago...

Oh, when will they ever learn?

WHERE HAVE ALL THE FLOWERS GONE?	
1961	PETE SEEGER

But everytime I read the papers...

We're waist deep in the big muddy

And the big fool says to push on

WAIST DEEP IN THE BIG MUDDY	
1967	PETE SEEGER

Pete Seeger, at a rally for Detente in

front of Carnegie Hall, New York.

AP/WIDE WORLD PHOTOS

The Seekers

You're always window shopping

But never stopping to buy

GEORGY GIRL	
1966	JIM DALE

To win in
we will
exter-
minate a

Bob Seger & The Silver Bullet Band

So you say he died for freedom

Well what if he died to save your lies

Go ahead and call me yellow

Two plus two is on my mind

2+2	
1968	BOB SEGER

Well, you walk into a restaurant strung out from the road

And you feel the eyes upon you as you're shakin' off the cold

You pretend it doesn't bother you but you just want to explode.

Most times you can't hear 'em talk, other times you can

All the same old cliches, "Is that a woman or a man?"

And you always seem outnumbered, you don't dare make a stand.

Out there in the spot light you're a million miles away

Every ounce of energy you try to give away

As the sweat pours out your body like the music that you play...

Here I am, on the road again. There I am up on the stage

Here I go playin' star again. There I go, turn the page.

TURN THE PAGE	
1973	**BOB SEGER**

He wants to dream like a young man

With the wisdom of an old man

He wants his home and security

He wants to live like a sailor at sea

Beautiful loser, where you gonna fall

When you realize you just don't need it all

He's your oldest and your best friend

If you need him, he'll be there again

He's always willing to be second best

A perfect lodger, a perfect guest

BEAUTIFUL LOSER	
1974, 1975	**BOB SEGER**

Sometimes even now when I'm feeling lonely and beat

I drift back in time and I find my feet

Down on Mainstreet

MAINSTREET	
1976	**BOB SEGER**

Vietnam, have to

nation.

DR. SPOCK, ON VIETNAM

243

⟶ 244

We weren't in love, oh no, far from it

We weren't searching for some pie in the sky summit

We were just young and restless and bored, living by the sword

And we'd steal away every chance we could

To the backroom, the alley, the trusty woods

I used her, she used me. But neither one cared

We were getting our share...

I woke last night to the sound of thunder

How far off, I sat and wondered

Started humming a song from 1962

Ain't it funny how the night moves

When you just don't seem to have as much to lose?

Strange how the night moves

With autumn closing in

NIGHT MOVES

1976　BOB SEGER

So you're a little bit older and a lot less bolder

Than you used to be

So you used to shake 'em down

But now you stop and think about your dignity

So now sweet sixteen has turned thirty one

You get to feelin' weary when the workday is done

All you got to do is get up into your kicks

If you're in a fix, come back baby

Rock and roll never forgets

ROCK AND ROLL NEVER FORGETS

1976　BOB SEGER

To teachers I'm just another child

To the IRS I'm just another file...

Gonna shout out at the ocean, "Hey, it's me"

I feel like a number

FEEL LIKE A NUMBER

1977　BOB SEGER

Somebody asked me what it's like to be beginning a third decade in rock n roll. The chance to play rock n roll as an adult feels like a privilege to me. I look at guys like Jagger and Springsteen to James Brown and Chuck Berry, and I figure they re damn nice company to be in. ● BOB SEGER

Wish I didn't know now what I didn't know then

We were young and we were strong; we were running

against the wind

AGAINST THE WIND

1980 | BOB SEGER

Sex Pistols

God save the Queen, the fascist regime...

We're the future, your future

GOD SAVE THE QUEEN	
1977	P. COOK, S. JONES, G. MATLOCK, J. ROTTEN

The Shangri-Las

I met him at the candy store...

That's when I fell for the leader of the pack

LEADER OF THE PACK	
1964	GEORGE MORTON, JEFF BARRY, ELLIE GREENWICH

Del Shannon

As I walk along I wonder

What went wrong with our love

A love that was so strong

RUNAWAY	
1961	DEL SHANNON, MAX CROOK

The Shirelles

Is this a lasting treasure

Or just a moment's pleasure...

Will you still love me tomorrow

WILL YOU LOVE ME TOMORROW	
1961	GERRY GOFFIN, CAROLE KING

Take my love with you

To any part of foreign shore...

I'll be true to you

SOLDIER BOY	
1962	FLORENCE GREEN, LUTHER DIXON

The Sex Pistols' Sid Vicious and Johnny Rotten performing in Atlanta, 1978.

UPI/BETTMANN

247

⟶ 248

The Silhouettes

After breakfast, ev'ryday

She throws the want ads right my way

And never fails to say, "Get a job"

GET A JOB	
1957	THE SILHOUETTES

Carly Simon

My friends from college they're all married now

They have their houses and their lawns...

Their children hate them for the things they're not

They hate themselves for what they are

But you say it's time we moved in together

And raised a family of our own, you and me

Well, that's the way I always heard it should be

THAT'S THE WAY I'VE ALWAYS HEARD IT SHOULD BE	
1970	CARLY SIMON, JACOB BRACKMAN

We can never know about the days to come

But we think about them anyway

And I wonder if I'm with you now

Or just chasing after some finer day

Anticipation is making me late

Is keeping me waiting...

Stay right here, 'cause these are the good old days

ANTICIPATION	
1971	CARLY SIMON

But a legend's only a lonely boy

When he goes home alone...

That isn't exactly what you had planned

LEGEND IN YOUR OWN TIME	
1971	CARLY SIMON

Carly Simon, performing on a television special.
AP/WIDE WORLD PHOTOS

In the name of honesty

In the name of what is fair

You always answer my questions

But they don't always answer my prayers

(WE HAVE) NO SECRETS

1972 | CARLY SIMON

I know you've had some bad luck with ladies before

They drove you or you drove them crazy

THE RIGHT THING TO DO

1972 | CARLY SIMON

You walked into the party like you were walking into a yacht

Your hat strategically dipped below one eye

Your scarf it was apricot

You had one eye in the mirror as you watched yourself gavotte...

You're so vain, you probably think this song is about you

YOU'RE SO VAIN

1972 | CARLY SIMON

All those crazy nights when I cried myself to sleep

Now melodrama never makes me weep anymore

'Cause I haven't got time for the pain...

Suffering was the only thing that made me feel I was alive

Thought that's just how much it cost to survive in this world

HAVEN'T GOT TIME FOR THE PAIN

1974 | CARLY SIMON, JACOB BRACKMAN

Let's make love for old time's sake

Let's set right an old mistake

Let's invite our hearts to break

It's right tonight

But just for old time's sake

FOR OLD TIME'S SAKE

1978 | CARLY SIMON

Paul Simon

Hello darkness my old friend

I've come to talk with you again

SOUND OF SILENCE

1964	PAUL SIMON

And a rock feels no pain

And an island never cries

I AM A ROCK

1965	PAUL SIMON

Got no deeds to do, no promises to keep

I'm dappled and drowsy and ready to sleep

THE 59TH STREET BRIDGE SONG (FEELIN' GROOVY)

1966	PAUL SIMON

I'm sittin' in a railway station ...

Homeward bound, I wish I was

HOMEWARD BOUND

1966	PAUL SIMON

Someone told me it's all happening at the zoo

I do believe it, I do believe it's true

AT THE ZOO

1967	PAUL SIMON

"Kathy, I'm lost," I said though I knew she was sleeping

"I'm empty and aching and I don't know why"

AMERICA

1968	PAUL SIMON

Father: Ben, what are you doing?
Ben (in the pool): Well, I'm just drifting.
Father: Then, may I ask, what was the point
of college and all that hard work?
Ben: Ya got me.

FROM THE 1969 FILM, THE GRADUATE

Where have you gone, Joe DiMaggio?

A nation turns its lonely eye to you

MRS. ROBINSON	
1968	**PAUL SIMON**

All lies in jest

Still a man hears what he wants to hear

And disregards the rest

THE BOXER	
1969	**PAUL SIMON**

Like a bridge over troubled water

I will lay me down

BRIDGE OVER TROUBLED WATER	
1969	**PAUL SIMON**

Cecilia, you're breaking my heart

You're shaking my confidence daily

CECILIA	
1969	**PAUL SIMON**

We come on the ship they call the Mayflower

We come on the ship that sails the moon

AMERICAN TUNE	
1973	**PAUL SIMON**

And we talked about some old times

And we drank ourselves some beers

STILL CRAZY AFTER ALL THESE YEARS	
1974	**PAUL SIMON**

Simon and Garfunkel's reunion performance in front of 500,000 fans in New York's Central Park, 1980.

UPI/BETTMANN

And then she kissed me

And I realized she probably was right

There must be fifty ways to leave your lover

FIFTY WAYS TO LEAVE YOUR LOVER	
1975	**PAUL SIMON**

God keeps his eye on us all

And he used to lean upon me

As I pledged allegiance to the wall

MY LITTLE TOWN	
1975	**PAUL SIMON**

A bad day is when I lie in bed

And think about what might have been

SLIP SLIDIN' AWAY	
1977	**PAUL SIMON**

Nancy Sinatra

These boots are made for walking

And that's just what they'll do

One of these days these boots

Are gonna walk all over you

Are you ready, boots? Start walking

THESE BOOTS	
1965	**LEE HAZLEWOOD**

Percy Sledge

When a man loves a woman

Can't keep his mind on nothin' else

WHEN A MAN LOVES A WOMAN	
1966	**C. LEWIS AND A. WRIGHT**

253

→ 254

Sly and the Family Stone

Gonna add a little gui-tar

To make it easy to move your feet

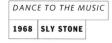

DANCE TO THE MUSIC	
1968	SLY STONE

Sometimes I'm right and I can be wrong

My own beliefs are in my song

EVERYDAY PEOPLE	
1968	SYLVESTER STEWART

Stand! Don't you know you are free

Well at least in your mind if you want to be

STAND	
1969	SLY STONE

I want to thank you falletin' me be mice elf again

THANK YOU (FALLETIN' ME BE MICE ELF AGAIN)	
1970	SLY STEWART

You can't cry cause you'll look broke down

But you're cryin' anyway cause you're all broke down

FAMILY AFFAIR	
1971	SLY STEWART

Oh, babies makin' babies

More and more, what's the score

BABIES MAKIN' BABIES	
1973	SYLVESTER STEWART

Patti Smith

They can't hurt you now

Because the night belongs to lovers

Because the night belongs to us

BECAUSE THE NIGHT	
1978	BRUCE SPRINGSTEEN

Sonny and Cher

They say we're young and we don't know

We won't find out until we grow...

They say our love won't pay the rent

Before it's earned our money's all been spent...

Babe, I got you babe

I GOT YOU BABE	
1965	SONNY BONO

The drums keep a-poundin' a rhythm to the brain

La di da di di La di da di da

THE BEAT GOES ON	
1967	SONNY BONO

Jimmy Soul

If you wanna be happy for the rest of your life

Don't make a pretty woman your wife

IF YOU WANT TO BE HAPPY	
1963	CARMELA GUIDA, FRANK GUIDA, JOSEPH ROYSTER

Spencer Davis Group

You better take it easy 'cause the place is on fire...

You got to gimme some lovin'

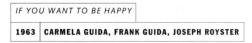

GIMME SOME LOVIN'	
1966	STEVE WINWOOD

I'm a man, yes I am

But I can't help but love you so

I'M A MAN	
1967	STEVE WINWOOD, JIMMY MILLER

Spiral Staircase

I love you more today than yesterday

But not as much as tomorrow

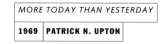

MORE TODAY THAN YESTERDAY	
1969	PATRICK N. UPTON

Spirit

Livin' in the city I've been abused...

Lookin' at my body I'm slippin' down, so far

The air I breathe and the water I drink

Selling me short and turning me around

ANIMAL ZOO	
1967	JAY FERGUSON

Love has found another way

I knew it would make it somehow

We will find a better way

LOVE HAS FOUND A WAY	
1967	RANDY CALIFORNIA, JOHN LOCKE

It's nature's way of receiving you

It's nature's way of retrieving you

It's nature's way of telling you

Something's wrong

NATURE'S WAY	
1967	RANDY CALIFORNIA

We got nothing to hide

We're married to the same bride

She eats away from inside

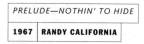

PRELUDE—NOTHIN' TO HIDE	
1967	**RANDY CALIFORNIA**

Come to the river bed

Got to tell you something

Go right to your head

I got a line on you

I GOT A LINE ON YOU	
1968	**RANDY CALIFORNIA**

Bruce Springsteen

I took month-long vacations in

The stratosphere and you know

It's really hard to hold your

Breath

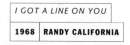

GROWIN' UP	
1972	**BRUCE SPRINGSTEEN**

They're breakin' beams and

crosses with a spastic's reelin' perfection...

Some storefront incarnation of

Maria, she's puttin' on me

The stare

And Bronx's best apostle stands

With his hand on his own hardware

LOST IN THE FLOOD	
1972	**BRUCE SPRINGSTEEN**

People deserve better. They deserve truth. They deserve honesty. The best music... is essentially there to provide you something to face the world with.

BRUCE SPRINGSTEEN

Princess cards she sends me
With her regards
Barroom eyes shine vacancy, to
See her you gotta look hard
And your strength is devastating
In the face of all these odds
Remember how I kept you
Waiting when it was my turn to
Be the god?...
So you left to find a better
Reason than the one we were
Living for
And it's not that nursery mouth
I came back for
It's not the way you're stretched
Out on the floor...
I came for you, for you, I came
For you, but you did not need
My urgency
I came for you, for you, I came
For you but your life was one
Long emergency
And your cloud line urges me

FOR YOU

| 1972 | BRUCE SPRINGSTEEN |

When I strut down the street
I could hear its heart beat
The sisters fell back and said
"Don't that man look pretty."
The cripple on the corner cried
Out, "Nickels for your pity."
Them gasoline boys downtown

Bruce Springsteen, one of the best live performers ever, on stage in St. Paul, Minnesota.

UPI/BETTMANN

259

⟶ 260

Sure talk gritty

It's so hard to be a saint in

The city...

I was the pimp's main prophet

I kept everything cool

Just a backstreet gambler

With the luck to lose...

The devil appeared like

Jesus through the steam in

The street

Showin' me a hand I knew even the

Cops couldn't beat

I felt his hot breath on my neck

As I dove into the heat

It's hard to be a saint when

You're just a boy out on

The street

And the sages of the subway

Sit just like the living dead

And the tracks clack out the

Rhythm, their eyes fixed

Straight ahead

They ride the line of balance

And hold on by just a thread...

You get up to get out at your

Next stop but they push you

Back down in your seat

Your heart starts beatin' faster

As you struggle to your feet

Then you're outa that hole

And back up on the street

And them south side sisters

Sure look pretty

The cripple on the corner cries

Out, "Nickels for your pity."...

It's so hard to be a saint

In the city

IT'S HARD TO BE A SAINT IN THE CITY	
1972	**BRUCE SPRINGSTEEN**

I think I really dug her 'cause

I was too loose to fake...

Together we moved like spirits

In the night

SPIRITS IN THE NIGHT	
1972	**BRUCE SPRINGSTEEN**

Rosalita jump a little higher

Senorita come sit by my fire...

Rosalita you're my stone desire

ROSALITA (COME OUT TONIGHT)	
1973	**BRUCE SPRINGSTEEN**

Mama always told me not to look

Into the sights of the sun

Oh but mama, that's where the fun is

BLINDED BY THE LIGHT	
1974	**BRUCE SPRINGSTEEN**

In the day we sweat it out in the streets

of a runaway American dream

At night we ride through mansions of

Glory in suicide machines...

Baby this town rips the bones from your back

It's a death trap, it's a suicide rap

We gotta get out while we're young

'Cause tramps like us, baby we were born to run...

The girls comb their hair in the rear-view mirrors

And the boys try to look so hard

The amusement park rises bold and stark

Kids are huddled on the beach in a mist...

The highways jammed with broken heroes

On a last chance power-drive

Everybody's out on the run tonight

But there's no place left to hide

Together, Wendy we can live with the sadness

Someday girl, I don't know when

We're gonna get to that place

Where we really want to go

And we'll walk in the sun

But till then tramps like us

Baby we were born to run

BORN TO RUN

1975 | BRUCE SPRINGSTEEN

Endless juke joints and Valentino drag

Where famous dancers scraped the tears

Up off the street dressed down in rags...

Laying here in the dark

You're like an angel on my chest

Just another tramp of hearts

Crying tears of faithlessness

Remember all the movies, Terry

We'd go to see

Trying to learn how to walk like the heroes

We thought we had to be

And after all this time

To find we're just like all the rest...

Hiding on the backstreets

BACKSTREETS

1975 | BRUCE SPRINGSTEEN

Barefoot girl sitting on the hood of a Dodge

Drinking warm beer in the soft summer rain...

They'll meet 'neath that giant Exxon sign

That brings this fair city light

Man there's an opera out on the Turnpike

There's a ballet being fought out in the alley...

In the tunnels uptown

The rat's own dream guns him down

As shots echo down them hallways in the night

No one watches as the ambulance pulls away

Or as the girl shuts out the bedroom light

Outside the street's on fire

In a real death waltz

Between what's flesh and what's fantasy

And the poets down here

Don't write nothing at all

They just stand back and let it all be

And in the quick of a knife

They reach for their moment

And try to make an honest stand

But they wind up wounded

Not even dead

Tonight in Jungleland

JUNGLELAND	
1975	**BRUCE SPRINGSTEEN**

And all we gotta do is hold up our end

Here stuff this in your pocket

It'll look like you're carrying a friend

And remember, just don't smile

Change your shirt, 'cause tonight we got style

Well Cherry says she's gonna walk

'Cause she found I took her radio and hocked it

But Eddie, man, she don't understand

⟶ 264

That two grand's practically sitting here in my pocket...

And tonight's going to be everything I said...

She'll see this time I wasn't just talking

Then I'm going to go out walking

Hey Eddie, can you catch us a ride

MEETING ACROSS THE RIVER

1975 | **BRUCE SPRINGSTEEN**

And the world is busting at its seams

And you're just a prisoner of your dreams

Holding on for your life...

You work nine to five

And somehow you survive

Till the night

NIGHT

1975 | **BRUCE SPRINGSTEEN**

That thunder in your heart

At night when you're kneeling in the dark

It says you're never going to leave her

But there's this angel in her eyes

That tells such desperate lies

And all you want to do is believe her.

And no matter where you sleep

Tonight or how far you run

Oh-o she's the one

SHE'S THE ONE

1975 | **BRUCE SPRINGSTEEN**

Seems like the whole world walking pretty

And you can't find the room to move

Well everybody better move over, that's all

'Cause I'm running on the bad side

And I got my back to the wall

Tenth Avenue freeze-out

TENTH AVENUE FREEZE-OUT	
1975	**BRUCE SPRINGSTEEN**

The screen door slams

Mary's dress waves

Like a vision she dances across the porch

As the radio plays

Roy Orbison singing for the lonely

Hey that's me and I want you only

Don't turn me home again

I just can't face myself alone again

Don't run back inside

Darling you know just what I'm here for

So you're scared and you're thinking

That maybe we ain't that young anymore

Show a little faith, there's magic in the night

You ain't a beauty, but hey you're alright

Oh and that's alright with me

You can hide 'neath your covers

And study your pain...

Well I got this guitar

And I learned how to make it talk

THUNDER ROAD	
1975	**BRUCE SPRINGSTEEN**

Talk about a dream, try to make it real

You wake up in the night with a fear so real

You spend your life waiting for a moment that just don't come

BADLANDS	
1978	**BRUCE SPRINGSTEEN**

Some folks are born into the good life

Other folks get it anyway, anyhow

I lost my money and I lost my wife

Them things don't seem to matter much to me now

Tonight I'll be on that hill 'cause I can't stop

I'll be on that hill with everything I got

Lives on the line where dreams are found or lost

I'll be there on time and I'll pay the cost

For wanting things that can only be found

In the darkness on the edge of town

Here's always a

DARKNESS ON THE EDGE OF TOWN	
1978	**BRUCE SPRINGSTEEN**

Blow away the dreams that break your heart

Blow away the lies that leave you nothing

But lost and broken hearted

THE PROMISED LAND	
1978	**BRUCE SPRINGSTEEN**

Got a wife and kids in Baltimore, Jack

I went out for a ride and I never went back

Like a river that don't know where it's goin'

I took a wrong turn and I just kept goin'

HUNGRY HEART	
1980	**BRUCE SPRINGSTEEN**

Now all those things that seemed so important

Well they just vanished right into the air

Now I just act like I don't remember

And Mary acts like she don't care.

But now those memories come back to haunt me

They haunt me like a curse

Is a dream a lie that don't come true

Or is it something worse

That brings me down to the river

Though I know the river is dry

THE RIVER	
1980	**BRUCE SPRINGSTEEN**

a song about blind faith. That is dangerous thing, whether it's your girlfriend... or your government.

BRUCE SPRINGSTEEN, IN CONCERT, 1984

Born down in a dead man's town

First kick I took was when I hit the ground

Ten years burnin' down the road

Nowhere to run, got nowhere to go

BORN IN THE USA	
1984	**BRUCE SPRINGSTEEN**

The walls of my room are closing in

There's a war outside still raging

You say it ain't ours anymore to win

NO SURRENDER	
1984	**BRUCE SPRINGSTEEN**

The Standells

Down by the river

Down by the banks of the river Charles

That's where you'll find it

Along with lovers, muggers, and thieves

I love that dirty water

Boston you're my home

Frustrated women, have to be in by twelve o'clock

But I'm wishin' and a hopin'

That just once that those doors weren't locked

DIRTY WATER	
1966	**ED COBB**

267

⟶ 268

Edwin Starr

War! Uh! What good is it for?

Absolutely nothin', say it again...

WAR	
1969	NORMAN WHITFIELD AND BARRETT STRONG

Kay Starr

Mom was dancing with Dad to my record machine...

They were trying to waltz to a rock and roll song

ROCK AND ROLL WALTZ	
1955	ROY ALFRED

Ringo Starr

You got to pay your dues

If you want to sing the blues

And you know it don't come easy

IT DON'T COME EASY	
1971	RINGO STARR

Steam

Na na na na na na na na

Hey hey hey goodbye

NA NA, HEY, HEY, KISS HIM GOODBYE	
1969	GARY DECARLO, DALE FRASHUER, PAUL LEKA

Steely Dan

All the time you know she's smiling

You'll be on your knees tomorrow

Yeah, you go back Jack, do it again

DO IT AGAIN	
1972	WALTER BECKER, DONALD BECKER

Well I hear the whistle, but I can't go

I'm gonna take her down to Mexico, I said

"Oh no, Guadalajara won't do."

MY OLD SCHOOL	
1973	**WALTER BECKER, DONALD FAGEN**

Are you reelin' in the years...

Are you gathering up the tears?

Have you had enough of mine?

REELIN' IN THE YEARS	
1973	**WALTER BECKER, DONALD FAGEN**

Those days are gone forever

Over a long time ago

PRETZEL LOGIC	
1974	**WALTER BECKER, DONALD FAGEN**

Aja, when all my dime dancin' is through

I run to you

AJA	
1977	**WALTER BECKER, DONALD FAGEN**

Break away, just when it seemed so clear...

Drink your big Black Cow

And get out of here

BLACK COW	
1977	**WALTER BECKER, DONALD FAGEN**

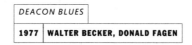

A victim of laughing chance

This is for me the essence of true romance

DEACON BLUES	
1977	**WALTER BECKER, DONALD FAGEN**

She's the raw flame, the live wire

She prays like a Roman

With her eyes on fire

JOSIE	
1977	**WALTER BECKER, DONALD FAGEN**

Steppenwolf

Get your motor running

Head out on the highway

Lookin' for adventure...

BORN TO BE WILD	
1968	**MARS BONFIRE**

I mean it's real hard to be free when you're bought and sold in the marketplace. Oh yeah, they're gonna talk to you and talk to you about individual freedom—but (when) they see a free individual, it's gonna scare 'em • JACK NICHOLSON IN THE 1969 FILM, <u>EASY RIDER</u>

Close your eyes girl

Look inside girl

Let the sound take you away

MAGIC CARPET RIDE	
1968	**MOREVE RUSHTON, JOHN KAY**

You know I've seen a lot of people walkin' around

With tombstones in their eyes...

I said God damn, the pusher man

THE PUSHER	
1968	**HOYT AXTON**

Cat Stevens

For you will still be here tomorrow

But your dreams may not

FATHER AND SON	
1970, 1971	**CAT STEVENS**

I'm looking for a hard headed woman

One who'll take me for myself...

One who'll make me do my best

And if I find that hard headed woman

I know the rest of my life will be blessed

HARD HEADED WOMAN	
1970, 1971	**CAT STEVENS**

And if I ever lose my eyes

If my color all runs dry

Then I won't have to cry no more

MOON SHADOW	
1970	**CAT STEVENS**

Now I've been smiling lately

Dreaming about the world as one...

Oh peace train, take this country

PEACE TRAIN	
1971	**CAT STEVENS**

Al Stewart

On a morning from a Bogart movie

In a picture where they turn back time

You go strolling through the crowd like Peter Lorre

YEAR OF THE CAT	
1976	**PETER WOOD, AL STEWART**

Rod Stewart

Wake up Maggie, I think I got something to say to you...

Maggie, I wish I'd never seen your face

MAGGIE MAY	
1971	**ROD STEWART, MARTIN QUITTENTON**

Knowing, that you lied straight-faced while I cried

Still I look to find a reason to believe

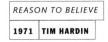

REASON TO BELIEVE	
1971	TIM HARDIN

I couldn't quote you no Dickens, Shelley, or Keats

'Cause it's all been said before

EVERY PICTURE TELLS A STORY	
1972	ROD STEWART

Something told me it was over

When I saw you and him talking

Something deep down in my soul said, "Cry boy"

When I saw you and him walking

I would rather, I would rather go blind, girl

Than to see you walk away from me...

I was just, I was just, I was just

Sitting here thinking

Of your kiss and your warm ways

When the reflection in the glass that I held to my lips, baby

Revealed the tears I had on my face

I would rather go blind, child

Than to see you walk away from me

I'D RATHER GO BLIND	
1972	BILLY FOSTER, ELLINGTON JORDAN

Wake Up Maggie: Rod Stewart

in concert.

AP/WIDE WORLD PHOTOS

The homesick blues and the radical views...

A little out of time, but I don't mind...

YOU WEAR IT WELL	
1972	MARTIN QUITTENTON

Don't say a word, my virgin child

Just let your inhibitions run wild...

Tonight's the night

TONIGHT'S THE NIGHT (IT'S GONNA BE ALRIGHT)	
1976	ROD STEWART

Cast out by the ones he loved

A victim of these gay days it seems...   There's been no

Oh Georgie stay; Don't go away

THE KILLING OF GEORGIE	
1977	ROD STEWART

Maybe, as a matter of fact I just can't grow up

Deep down ain't we all a little juvenile

AIN'T LOVE A BITCH	
1978	ROD STEWART, GARY GRAINGER

If ya want my money

And you think I'm sexy

Come on honey tell me so

DO (DA) YA THINK I'M SEXY	
1978	ROD STEWART, CARMINE APPICE

You got legs right up to your neck

You're making me a physical wreck

HOT LEGS	
1978	ROD STEWART

Stephen Stills

If you can't be with the one you love

Love the one you're with

LOVE THE ONE YOU'RE WITH	
1970	STEPHEN STILLS

Strawberry Alarm Clock

Who cares what games we choose

Little to win, but nothing to lose

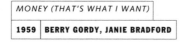

INCENSE AND PEPPERMINTS	
1967	JOHN CARTER, TIM GILBERT

top authority saying what marijuana does to you. I really don't know that much about it. I tried it once, but it didn't do anything to me. JOHN WAYNE

Barrett Strong

Money don't get everything it's true

But what it don't get I can't use

MONEY (THAT'S WHAT I WANT)	
1959	BERRY GORDY, JANIE BRADFORD

Styx

Reflections in the waves start my memories

Some happy, some sad

I think of childhood friends and the dreams we had

COME SAIL AWAY	
1977	DENNIS DE YOUNG

Sugarloaf

Green-eyed lady, ocean lady

Child of nature, friend of man

GREEN-EYED LADY	
1970	JERRY CORBETTA, J.C. PHILLIPS, DAVID RIORDAN

275

⟶ 276

Donna Summer

Someone left a cake out in the rain

I don't think that I can take it

'Cause it took so long to bake it

MACARTHUR PARK	
1968	JIMMY WEBB

Supertramp

You say it all depends on money

And who is in your family tree

Right, right, you're bloody well right

BLOODY WELL RIGHT	
1974	ROGER HODGSON, RICHARD DAVIES

The Supremes

Love is like an itching in my heart...

And baby I can't scratch it

LOVE IS LIKE AN ITCHING IN MY HEART	
1966	EDDIE HOLLAND, LAMONT DOZIER, BRIAN HOLLAND

Set me free why don't you baby

Get out of my life why don't you baby?

YOU KEEP ME HANGIN' ON	
1966	BRIAN HOLLAND, LAMONT DOZIER, EDWARD HOLLAND, JR.

Love child, never meant to be

Love child, born in poverty...

Take a look at me

LOVE CHILD	
1968	PAM SAWYER, R. DEAN TAYLOR, FRANK WILSON, DEKE RICHARDS

Don't you wanna go up the ladder to the roof

Where we can see heaven much better

UP THE LADDER TO THE ROOF	
1970	VINCENT DIMIRCO, FRANK WILSON

The Swinging Medallions

Woke up this morning my head was so bad

The worst hangover that I ever had

What happened to me last night

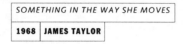

DOUBLE SHOT (OF MY BABY'S LOVE)	
1966	DON SMITH, CYRIL E. VETTER

James Taylor

She has the power to go

Where no one else can find me

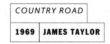

SOMETHING IN THE WAY SHE MOVES	
1968	JAMES TAYLOR

I guess my feet know where they want me to go

Walkin' on a country road

COUNTRY ROAD	
1969	JAMES TAYLOR

Won't you look down upon me Jesus

You've got to help me make a stand

You've got to see me through another day

FIRE AND RAIN	
1969	JAMES TAYLOR

Do me wrong, do me right

Tell me lies, but hold me tight...

But don't let me be lonely tonight

DON'T LET ME BE LONELY TONIGHT	
1973	JAMES TAYLOR

Johnny Taylor

Who's makin' love to your old lady

While you are out makin' love?

WHO'S MAKING LOVE	
1968	BETTY CRUTCHER, DON DAVIS, AL JACKSON

The Temptations

But after I've been crying all night

The sun is cold and the new day seems old

SINCE I LOST MY BABY	
1965	WILLIAM ROBINSON, WARREN MOORE

I know you wanna leave me

But I refuse to let you go

AIN'T TOO PROUD TO BEG	
1966	NORMAN WHITFIELD, EDDIE HOLLAND

Your touch, your touch has gone cold...

I can feel the presence of another man

(I KNOW) I'M LOSING YOU	
1966	NORMAN WHITFIELD, EDDIE HOLLAND, CORNELIUS GRANT

You can be what you wanna be

You ain't got no responsibility

Up, up and away, on Cloud Nine

CLOUD NINE	
1968	BARRETT STRONG, NORMAN WHITFIELD

I know to you it might sound strange

But I wish it would rain

I WISH IT WOULD RAIN	
1968	NORMAN WHITFIELD, BARRETT STRONG, ROGER PENZABENE

Evolution, revolution, gun control, the sound of soul

Shooting rockets to the moon, kids growing up too soon

BALL OF CONFUSION	
1970	NORMAN WHITFIELD AND BARRETT STRONG

To add to their misery they had little hope of, deliverance. For where does one run to when he's already in the promised land? CLAUDE BROWN IN "MANCHILD IN THE PROMISED LAND"

Psychadelic Shack

That's where it's at

PSYCHEDELIC SHACK	
1970	BARRETT STRONG, NORMAN WHITFIELD

It was just my imagination (once again)

Running away with me

JUST MY IMAGINATION	
1971	NORMAN WHITFIELD, BARRETT STRONG

Papa was a rolling stone

Wherever he laid his hat was his home

And when he died all he left us was alone

PAPA WAS A ROLLING STONE	
1972	NORMAN WHITFIELD, BARRETT STRONG

Ten Years After

Look out baby I'm comin' to get you

One more time, goin' home

GOIN' HOME	
1969	TRADITIONAL

George Thorogood and the Destroyers

I broke a thousand hearts before I met you

I'll break a thousand more before I'm through...

I'm b-b-b-b-bad

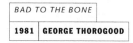

BAD TO THE BONE	
1981	GEORGE THOROGOOD

You know when I drink alone

I prefer to be by myself

I DRINK ALONE	
1985	GEORGE THOROGOOD

Three Dog Night

Eli's comin' hide your heart girl

Girl, Eli's a' comin' you'd better go

ELI'S COMING	
1968	LAURA NYRO

It's just no good anymore since she went away

Now I spend my time just makin' rhymes of yesterday

ONE	
1968	HARRY NILSSON

Especially people who care about strangers...

Do you only care about the bleeding crowd?

EASY TO BE HARD	
1969	GEROME RAGNI, JAMES RADO

Jeremiah was a bullfrog

Was a good friend of mine

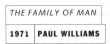

JOY TO THE WORLD	
1970	HOYT AXTON

Well, I never been to Spain...

They say the ladies are insane there

And they sure know how to use it

NEVER BEEN TO SPAIN	
1970	HOYT AXTON

This tired city was somebody's dream

Billboard horizons as black as they seem

THE FAMILY OF MAN	
1971	PAUL WILLIAMS

Thunderclap Newton

The revolution's near and you know that it's right...

We have got to get it together right now

SOMETHING IN THE AIR	
1969	SPEEDY KEEN

(Rubin) and Abbie (Hoffman) couldn't organize a luncheon—much less a revolution. **MARSHALL ROSENTHAL**

Traffic

Dear Mister Fantasy play us a tune

Something to make us all happy

DEAR MR. FANTASY	
1967	STEVE WINWOOD

Take extra care not to lose what you feel

The apple you're eating is simple and real...

Guiding your visions to heaven

And heaven is in your mind

HEAVEN IS IN YOUR MIND	
1967	STEVE WINWOOD, JAMES CAPALDI, CHRIS WOOD

'Cause Molly made a stew that'll make a new girl out of you

So follow me, it's good for you

That good old fashioned medicated goo

MEDICATED GOO	
1968	STEVE WINWOOD, JIMMY MILLER

You are the reason I've been waiting all these years

Somebody holds the key...

I'm wasted and I can't find my way home

CAN'T FIND MY WAY HOME	
1969	STEVE WINWOOD

281

⟶ 282

And the man in the suit

Has just bought a new car

From the profit he made on your dreams

LOW SPARK OF HIGH-HEELED BOYS	
1972	STEVE WINWOOD, JIM CAPALDI

The Troggs

Wild thing, I think I love you

But I wanna know for sure

WILD THING	
1966	CHIP TAYLOR

Tina Turner

What's love got to do with it

What's love, but a second-hand emotion

WHAT'S LOVE GOT TO DO WITH IT	
1984	TERRY BRITTEN, GRAHAM LYLE

The Turtles

Imagine me and you, I do

I think about you day and night

HAPPY TOGETHER	
1966	ALAN GORDON, GARRY BONNER

Me oh my lucky guy is what I am

Tell you why you'll understand

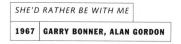

SHE'D RATHER BE WITH ME	
1967	GARRY BONNER, ALAN GORDON

Ritchie Valens

Para bailar La Bamba...

Se nessi una poca de gracia

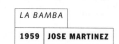

LA BAMBA	
1959	JOSE MARTINEZ

Frankie Valli

I love you, baby (and if it's quite alright)

I need you baby

CAN'T TAKE MY EYES OFF YOU	
1967	BOB CREWE, BOB GAUDIO

Van Halen

Ooh baby baby...

You're old enough to

Dance the night away

DANCE THE NIGHT AWAY	
1979	DAVID LEE ROTH, MICHAEL SOBOLEWSKI, ALEX VAN HALEN, EDWARD VAN HALEN

Gene Vincent

Be-bop-a-Lula, she's my baby

Be-bop-a-Lula, I don't mean maybe

BE-BOP-A-LULA	
1956	GENE VINCENT, TEX DAVIS

Loudon Wainwright III

Dead skunk in the middle of the road

And it's stinkin' to high heaven

DEAD SKUNK	
1973	LOUDON WAINWRIGHT III

Jerry Jeff Walker

He said his name, Bojangles

Then he dance a lick across the cell

He grabbed his pants a better stance

Oh, he jumped up high...

Mr. Bojangles, Mr. Bojangles

Mr. Bojangles—dance

MR. BOJANGLES	
1968	JERRY JEFF WALKER

Dionne Warwick

What's it all about Alfie?

Is it just for the moment we live...

Or are we meant to be kind?

ALFIE	
1966	**HAL DAVID**

Joe Walsh

Well he's tellin' us this and he's tellin us that

Changin' it every day

Says it doesn't matter

ROCKY MOUNTAIN WAY	
1973	**JOE WALSH, JOEY VITALE, KENNY PASSARELLI, ROCHE GRACE**

I go to parties, sometimes until four

It's hard to leave when you can't find the door

It's tough to handle this fortune and fame

Everybody's so different, I haven't changed

Lucky I'm sane after all I've been through

I can't complain, but sometimes I still do

Life's been good to me so far

LIFE'S BEEN GOOD TO ME	
1978	**JOE WALSH**

Billy Ward and the Dominoes

Fifteen minutes of kissin'

And then you'll holler, "Please don't stop"

There'll be fifteen minutes of teasin'

Fifteen minutes of squeezin', and

Fifteen minutes of blowin' my top

SIXTY MINUTE MAN	
1951	**BILLY WARD, ROSE MARKS**

The Who

People try to put us down...

Things they do look awful cold

Hope I die before I get old

> *MY GENERATION*
>
> **1965** | **PETE TOWNSHEND**

Substitute you for my mum

At least I get my washing done

> *SUBSTITUTE*
>
> **1966** | **PETE TOWNSHEND**

I know you deceived me, now here's a surprise

I know that you have, 'cause there's magic in my eyes

> *I CAN SEE FOR MILES*
>
> **1967** | **PETE TOWNSHEND**

I'm the gypsy, the acid Queen

Pay before we start

The gypsy, I'm guaranteed

To tear your soul apart...

Give us a room, close the door

Leave us for awhile

Your boy won't be a boy no more

Young, but not a child...

My work is done, now look at him

He's never been more alive

His head it shakes, his fingers clutch

Watch his body writhe...

I'm the gypsy, I'm guaranteed

To break your little heart

> *ACID QUEEN*
>
> **1969** | **PETE TOWNSHEND**

Sickness will surely take the mind

Where minds can't usually go

Come on amazing journey

And learn all you should know

AMAZING JOURNEY

1969 | **PETE TOWNSHEND**

Did you ever see the faces of the children?

They get so excited

Waking up on Christmas morning

Hours before the winter sun's ignited

And Tommy doesn't know what day it is

He doesn't know who Jesus was or what praying is

How can he be saved

From the eternal grave?

CHRISTMAS

1969 | **PETE TOWNSHEND**

Let's think of a game to play

Now the grown ups have all gone away

You won't be much fun

Being blind, deaf, and dumb

But I've no one to play with today

Do you know how to play hide and seek?

To find me it would take you a week

But tied to that chair

You won't go anywhere

There's a lot I can do with a freak

COUSIN KEVIN

1969 | **JOHN ENTWISTLE**

He seems to be completely unreceptive

The test I gave him show no sense at all...

There is no chance, no untried operation

All hope lies with him and none with me

Imagine though the shock from isolation

When he suddenly can hear and speak and see

See me, feel me

Touch me, heal me...

Go to the mirror boy

Go to the mirror boy

I often wonder what he is feeling

Has he ever heard a word I've said?

Look at him in the mirror dreaming

What is happening in his head?

Listening to you I get the music

Gazing at you I get the heat

Following you I climb the mountain

I get excitement at your feet

Right behind you I get the millions

Oh you I see the glory

From you I get opinions

From you I get the story

What is happening in his head?

Oh, I wish I knew

I wish I knew

GO TO THE MIRROR	
1969	**PETE TOWNSHEND**

I'm free, I'm free

And freedom tastes of reality

I'M FREE	
1969	**PETE TOWNSHEND**

My great pride has always been that I'm writing for a group of people that commissioned me back in 1963. I'm still trying to find a way of saying what they want to say. If I can stay in touch with that, then I hang on to my roots. In that sense, rock-and-roll is important because I'm still doing the job that I did in 1963 when I wrote the first few Who songs. And if I'm still working for that bunch of people, then I'm still in touch with that continuum and it doesn't really matter how I do it.

PETE TOWNSHEND

Pete Townshend gives one of his trademark jumps during a performance of the rock-opera "Tommy" at the Metropolitan Opera House in 1970.

UPI/BETTMANN

Roger Daltrey and Pete Townshend
of The Who.

UPI/BETTMANN

Ever since I was a young boy

I played the silver ball

From Soho down to Brighton

I must have played 'em all

But I ain't seen nothin' like him

In any amusement hall

That deaf, dumb, and blind kid

Sure plays a mean pinball

PINBALL WIZARD	
1969	PETE TOWNSHEND

Gotta feeling twenty one

Is gonna be a good year

Especially if you and me

See it in together...

I've got no reason

To be over optimistic

But somehow when you smile

I can brave bad weather

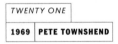

TWENTY ONE	
1969	PETE TOWNSHEND

You'll feel me coming

A new vibration

From far you'll see me;

I'm a sensation

SENSATION	
1969	PETE TOWNSHEND

You don't answer my call

With even a nod or a twitch

But you gaze at your own reflection (alright!)

You don't seem to see me

But I think you can see myself

How can the mirror affect you?

SMASH THE MIRROR	
1969	PETE TOWNSHEND

Welcome to the camp

I guess you all know why we're here

My name is Tommy

And became aware this year...

We're not gonna take it

Never did and never will

Don't want no religion

And as far as we can tell

We're not gonna take you

We forsake you

Gonna rape you

Let's forget you better still

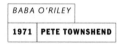

WE'RE NOT GONNA TAKE IT

1969	PETE TOWNSHEND

I don't need to fight

To prove I'm right

I don't need to be forgiven

Don't cry

Don't raise your eye

It's only teenage wasteland

BABA O'RILEY

1971	PETE TOWNSHEND

I'd pay any price just to get you

I'd work all my life and I will to win you

I'd stand naked, stoned and stabbed

I'd call that a bargain;

The best I ever had...

I sit lookin' round;

I look at my face in the mirror

I know I'm worth nothing without you

And like, one and one don't make two

One and one make one

And I'm looking for that free ride to me;

I'm looking for you

BARGAIN

1971 PETE TOWNSHEND

But my dreams

They aren't as empty

As my conscience seems to be...

If I swallow anything evil

Put your finger down my throat

And if I shiver please give me a blanket

Keep me warm, let me wear your coat

BEHIND BLUE EYES

1971 PETE TOWNSHEND

I don't care about pollution

I'm an air conditioned gypsy

That's my solution:

Watch the police and tax-man miss me

I'm mobile!

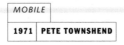

MOBILE

1971 PETE TOWNSHEND

There once was a note

Pure and easy

Playing so free

Like a breath rippling by

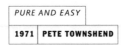

PURE AND EASY

1971 PETE TOWNSHEND

The song is over

I'm left with only tears

I must remember

Even if it takes a million years...

THE SONG IS OVER	
1971	PETE TOWNSHEND

I'll tip my hat to the new constitution

Take a bow for the new revolution

Smile and grin at the change all around

Pick up my guitar and play

Just like yesterday

And I'll get on my knees and pray

We don't get fooled again

The change it had to come

We knew it all along

We were liberated from the fold, that's all

The world looks just the same

And history ain't blamed

'Cause the banners all were flown in the last war...

Meet the new boss

Same as the old boss

WON'T GET FOOLED AGAIN	
1971	PETE TOWNSHEND

Long live rock come on and join the line

Long live rock, be it dead or alive

LONG LIVE ROCK	
1972	PETE TOWNSHEND

I see a man without a problem

I see a country always starved

Is it in my head?

IS IT IN MY HEAD?	
1973	PETE TOWNSHEND

→ 294

Wild Cherry

Play that funky music

White boy

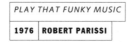

PLAY THAT FUNKY MUSIC	
1976	ROBERT PARISSI

Larry Williams

You make me dizzy Miss Lizzy

The way you rock and roll...

C'mon Miss Lizzy

Love me before I grow too old

DIZZY MISS LIZZY	
1958	LARRY WILLIAMS

A bad little kid moved into my neighborhood

He won't do nothing right, his report card looks no good

He don't want to go to school and learn to read and write

He sits around the house and plays that

Rock and roll music all night

BAD BOY	
1959	LARRY WILLIAMS

Chuck Willis

They say that rock and roll will soon fade away

But I just wanna tell ya, rock and roll is here to stay

HANG UP MY ROCK AND ROLL SHOES	
1958, 1972	CHUCK WILLIS

Frank J. Wilson and the Cavaliers

Where oh where can my baby be

The Lord took her away from me

She's gone to heaven so I got to be good

LAST KISS	
1964	WAYNE COCHRAN

The Winstons

He says education is the thing

If you want to compete

Because without it son life ain't very sweet

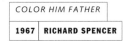

COLOR HIM FATHER	
1967	RICHARD SPENCER

Edgar Winter

Rock 'n roll hootchie koo

Lawdy mama, light my fuse

ROCK AND ROLL HOOTCHIE KOO	
1974	RICK DERRINGER

Stevie Wonder

For once I can touch what my heart used to dream of

FOR ONCE IN MY LIFE	
1965	RONALD MILLER

Powers keep on lyin'

While your people keep on dyin'...

Cause it won't be too long

HIGHER GROUND	
1973	STEVIE WONDER

His patience's long, but soon he won't have any...

Livin' just enough, just enough, for the city

LIVING FOR THE CITY	
1973	STEVIE WONDER

I'm too high, I'm too high

But I ain't touched the sky

TOO HIGH	
1973	STEVIE WONDER

Would you like to go with me
Down my dead end street?

VILLAGE GHETTO LAND	
1976	STEVIE WONDER, BYRD

Stevie Wonder in 1967 when he was known as
"Little Stevie Wonder."

UPI/BETTMANN

The Yardbirds

Come tomorrow, will I be older?

Come tomorrow, maybe a soldier

SHAPES OF THINGS	
1966	**PAUL SAMWELL-SMITH, KEITH RELF, JIM McCARTY**

Yes

The goal is to capture only one

Don't surround yourself with yourself

Move on back a square

YOUR MOVE/I'VE SEEN ALL GOOD PEOPLE	
1971	**JON ANDERSON, CHRIS SQUIRE**

On a sailing ship to nowhere leaving anyplace

If the summer changed to winter yours is no disgrace

YOURS IS NO DISGRACE	
1972	**JON ANDERSON**

Neil Young

I saw cotton and I saw black

Tall white mansions and little shacks

SOUTHERN MAN	
1970	**NEIL YOUNG**

When you dance

Do your senses tingle

And take a chance

WHEN YOU DANCE	
1970	**NEIL YOUNG**

See the old folks, tied in white robes

Hear the banjos don't it take you down home

ALABAMA	
1972	**NEIL YOUNG**

I caught you knocking at my cellar door

I love you, baby, can I have some more?

Ooh, the damage done

THE NEEDLE AND THE DAMAGE DONE	
1972	NEIL YOUNG

Old man, take a look at my life

I'm a lot like you were

OLD MAN	
1972	NEIL YOUNG

The Young Rascals

I was feelin' somethin' bad

I asked my family doctor just what I had

I said "Doctor, Mr. M.D.

Can you tell me what's ailing me?"

He said... all I really need is good lovin

I got the fever, you got the cure

Good lovin'

GOOD LOVIN'	
1965	RUDY CLARK, ARTHUR RESNICK

How can I be sure

In a world that's constantly changing

HOW CAN I BE SURE?	
1967	FELIX CAVALIERE, EDWARD BRIGATI, JR.

The Youngbloods

Everybody get together

Try to love one another right now

GET TOGETHER	
1967	DINO VALENTI

Frank Zappa and the Mothers of Invention

What's the ugliest part of your body?...

But I think it's your mind!

WHAT'S THE UGLIEST PART OF YOUR BODY?
1968 | **FRANK ZAPPA**

in this ,room is wearing a
and don't kid yourself.

FRANK ZAPPA

Every town must have a place

Where phony hippies meet

Psychadelic dungeons popping up on every street

WHO NEEDS THE PEACE CORPS?
1968 | **FRANK ZAPPA**

Watch out where the huskies go

Don't you eat the yellow snow

DON'T EAT THE YELLOW SNOW
1973 | **FRANK ZAPPA**

They has a fit while I commit

My social suicide, I'm a

dancin' fool

DANCIN' FOOL
1975 | **FRANK ZAPPA**

Speed will turn you into your parents.

FRANK ZAPPA

I wanna nasty little Jewish princess

Who don't know shit about cooking

And is arrogant looking

JEWISH PRINCESS
1979 | **FRANK ZAPPA**

299

⟶ 300

Rock journalism is people who can't write interviewing people who can't talk for people who can't read.

FRANK ZAPPA

Warren Zevon

I saw a werewolf drinking a pina colada at Trader Vic's

His hair was perfect

Werewolves of London

WEREWOLVES OF LONDON	
1975	LEROY P. MARINELL, WADDY WACHTEL, WARREN ZEVON

He took little Suzie to the junior prom

And he raped her and killed her

Then he took her home

Excitable boy, they all said

EXCITABLE BOY	
1976	LEROY P. MARINELL, WARREN ZEVON

She's so many women, he can't find the one

Who was his friend

HASTEN DOWN THE WIND	
1977	WARREN ZEVON

Never thought I'd have to pay so dearly

For what was already mine

Accidentally like a martyr

The hurt gets worse and the heart gets harder

ACCIDENTALLY LIKE A MARTYR	
1978	WARREN ZEVON

I went home with a waitress

The way I always do

How was I to know

She was with the Russians, too

I'm down on my luck...

Send lawyers, guns, and money

LAWERS, GUNS, AND MONEY	
1978	WARREN ZEVON

Frank Zappa, on guitar, mocked many of the popular rock conventions with his acid-tongued lyrics and unique musical style.

301

⟶ 302

They say Jesus will find you wherever you go

But when he'll come looking for you, they don't know

GORILLA, YOU'RE A DESPERADO	
1980	WARREN ZEVON

The Zombies

Well no one told me about her

(What could I do)

Nobody told me about her

(Though they all knew)

It's too late to say you're sorry

(How would I know, why should I care)

Please don't bother tryin' to find her

She's not there

Well, let me tell you about the way she looked

SHE'S NOT THERE	
1964	ROD ARGENT

What's your name, who's your daddy

Is he rich like me?

Has he taken any time

To show you what you need to live

TIME OF THE SEASON	
1967	ROD ARGENT

Zager and Evans

In the year 3535

Ain't gonna need to tell the truth, tell no lies

Everything you think, do, or say

Is in the pill you took today...

In the year 6565

Ain't gonna need no husband, won't need no wives

You'll pick your sons, pick your daughter too

From the bottom of a long glass tube, whoah, whoah...

In the year 9595

I'm kinda wondering if man is gonna be alive

He's taken everything this old earth can give

And he ain't put back nothin' whoah, whoah

Now it's been ten thousand years

Man has cried a billion tears

For what he never knew

Now man's reign is through

But through eternal night

The twinkling of starlight

So very far away

Maybe it was only yesterday

IN THE YEAR 2525	
1969	**RICK EVANS**

ZZ Top

I ain't askin' for much

I said Lord take me downtown

I'm just lookin' for some tush

TUSH	
1975, 1978	**BILLY GIBBONS, FRANK BEARD, DUSTY HILL**

I got a girl she lives on the hill

She won't do it but her sister will

She do the tube snake boogie

TUBE SNAKE BOOGIE	
1981	**BILLY GIBBONS, FRANK BEARD, DUSTY HILL**

303

⟶ 304

Songtitle and Keyword Index

Songwriter Index

Song Lyric Acknowledgments

315

⟶ 316